THE LAKE DISTRICT
Landscape Heritage

THE LAKE DISTRICT
Landscape Heritage

Edited by William Rollinson

Series Editor:
Allan Patmore

CONTRIBUTORS

Tom Clare
David Shotter
Ian Whyte
Angus Winchester
Andrew Lowe
Paul Hindle
R. W. Brunskill
William Rollinson

DAVID & CHARLES
Newton Abbot   London

ACKNOWLEDGEMENTS

The authors would like to express their sincere thanks to the following for help in writing and production of this book:

Wilfred Blackburn, Jane Campbell, Christine Denmead, Gustav Dobrzynski, David Fawcett, Yvonne Gray, Alan Hodgkiss, Philip Howard, Pat Kitchen, The Lake District National Park Planning Board, Peter Mingins, The National Trust, Colin Shelbourn and the Westmorland Gazette.

Page 2 Crummock Water *(Simon Crouch)*

British Library Cataloguing in Publication Data
The Lake District: landscape heritage.
1. Cumbria. Lake District. Landscape, to 1988
I. Rollinson, William, *1937-*
719'.09427'8

ISBN 0-7153-9077-5

Phototypeset by ABM Typographics Limited, Hull
and printed in Great Britain
by Redwood Burn Limited, Trowbridge
for David & Charles Publishers plc
Brunel House   Newton Abbot   Devon

CONTENTS

INTRODUCTION

Few places in Britain have such a rich and varied landscape as the Lake District. Here the Romantic Movement had its origins and the mountains, dales, lakes and rivers which inspired Wordsworth and Coleridge, Turner and Constable are today visited by countless thousands of tourists. Even the most car-confined tripper can scarcely fail to be moved by the play of light and shade on farm and fell, by the wraith-like mists shrouding forest and mere, or by the westering sun on bracken slopes and rock faces. Yet there is a common misconception that this landscape is somehow 'natural', a timeless environment which is fundamentally the same today as that witnessed by our Neolithic ancestors some five thousand years ago. Nothing could be further from the truth, for this is largely an artificial environment, constantly changing under the influence of man and his activities – and everywhere man's signature on this landscape is clear and legible for those who are able to decipher it. Here Iron Age settlers built their villages and animal compounds, Roman legions stamped their indelible mark in the form of forts and well-engineered roads. Norse settlers foraged up the dales, felling forests and establishing farmsteads and saeters, leaving their place-names – becks, slacks, gills and thwaites – scotched on the fellsides.

Warfare has also left its mark ; Norman motte-and-baileys, stone keeps, stoutly-built pele towers designed to keep out marauding Scots are gaunt reminders of Cumbria's often turbulent history. The Age of Improvement finds expression in the newly-built stone farmhouses and in the planned landscapes of Parliamentary enclosure, while the drystone walls, snaking and dipping over the highest fells, are an eloquent testimony not only to the reclamation of the fells but also to the fortitude of the remarkable men who built them. In the uplands, the overgrown spoil tips and fenced-off shafts of former copper workings are evidence of the impact of industrial man on the landscape. The change and challenge of this developing landscape continues; the insistent, ruler-straight outlines of dark coniferous forests, and the silent

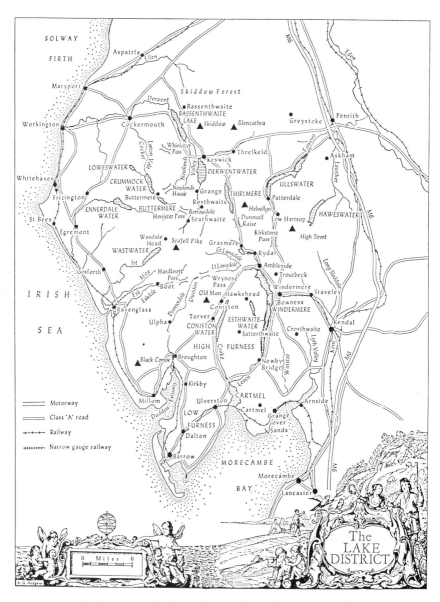

Fig 1 A map of the Lake District, drawn by A. G. Hodgkiss.

reservoirs and large, yet overcrowded, car parks are twentieth-century man's contribution to the landscape.

This book explores all these aspects of the landscape heritage of the Lake District; it has been written by acknowledged experts in their fields who, together, tell the story of the Lake District landscape from the Neolithic to the National Park.

8

1
THE PREHISTORIC
LANDSCAPE

THERE is no evidence for man in the Lake District before the end of the last Ice Age, if only because the ice would have scoured away any surface remains. At the time of the Allerød interstadial c10000–8500bc, however, the landscape was not dissimilar from parts of Norway today: corrie glaciers between jagged peaks; barren expanses of rock, morraine and outwash; tundra type flora and fauna and perhaps, on the fringes of the area, a few strands of birch trees. Included in the fauna were reindeer and it was probably the herds of this animal that attracted the first men to the area.

Flints belonging to one such *Upper Palaeolithic* group, together with a portion of reindeer antler, have been recovered from Kirkhead Cave near Grange, and flints of possibly similar date have now been re-covered from another cave not far away. The location of both sites suggests these early hunting communities were operating on the fringes of the Lake District, although the contemporary coastline is unknown. We might, however, surmise that they visited the area on a seasonal basis and at that time of year, probably summer, when the wildlife (animal and vegetable) was most abundant.

The onset of poorer climatic conditions and associated changes in the available flora and fauna seem to have led to the abandonment of Kirkhead cave. After 8000bc, however, the climate steadily improved until, about 5000bc, it reached its optimum with forest covering perhaps 90% of the land – deciduous forest on well drained ground with strands of birch and pine in less favoured localities such as the fell tops. It is, however, not clear at what height the continuous tree cover stopped, some estimates being that the mountains were largely un-forested above 2500ft (762.5m). Although we can assume conditions were favourable for human occupation several millennia before the climatic optimum, we have no certain evidence for renewed human activity before 6000bc. The flints left by these new, *Mesolithic*, communities are very small and usually called microliths. Not surprisingly, they are often missed by the untrained eye and what we know of these people in the Lake District is largely thanks to the work of one amateur archaeologist; indeed it might be said that the distribution of mesolithic man in the Lake District is the distribution of one man's fieldwork.

Microliths have, however, not been found everywhere and we can be reasonably confident that these hunting and food gathering peoples preferred those areas where the forest canopy was less dense and where there was a good supply of beach flint or chert for tools. Perhaps the best picture we have comes from Eskmeals, south of Ravenglass. There, after 7000–6500bc, there was a shallow brackish lagoon parallel to the coast and separated from the sea by a sandbar. The sea afforded fish and shellfish, the lagoon other types of fish and wildfowl, the River Esk salmon and trout in season, and the dry land and higher slopes bigger game, nuts, berries and other edible plants. So rich was the potential food supply within a few miles of Eskmeals it would have been possible for the mesolithic community to have been permanently established in the area rather than itinerant.

Nevertheless within the forested, mesolithic landscape grazing was always in short supply and not unnaturally the game tended to move to or gather wherever it, and in particular open grassland, was to be found. In general, natural grassland would have been available along the fluctuating margins of water (the sea, some lakes and floodplains), on mountain tops or steep slopes where tree cover was thin or non-existent, or wherever trees blew down and opened up the forest canopy. Such areas, amongst which we should include Eskmeals, would be a natural focus for game and thus also attractive to human communities.

From about 4000bc onwards some of these early forest clearings are associated in the pollen record with charcoal. One interpretation is that natural fires were opening up small areas of the forest and producing pockets of grassland. An alternative theory, however, is that the fires were deliberately created by man to produce grassland to attract wild herds and thus make hunting easier. It has, for example, been suggested that at Eskmeals elm leaves were being gathered in an attempt to circumvent the natural, periodical, local scarcity of animal feed which would have led to the animals migrating. It is, therefore, a moot point whether by the time the first 'farmers' arrived the mesolithic people were already clearing some areas of forest and herding and managing animals much as the Lapps can be said to 'manage' 'wild' reindeer. As such the transition from a hunting/food gathering

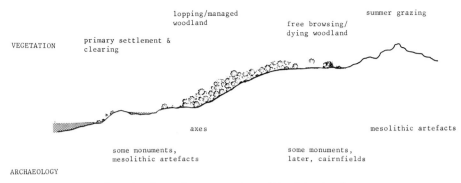

VEGETATION

lopping/managed
woodland

summer grazing

free browsing/
dying woodland

primary settlement &
clearing

axes

mesolithic artefacts

some monuments,
mesolithic artefacts

some monuments,
later, cairnfields

ARCHAEOLOGY

Fig 2 A schematic cross section of Neolithic land use

economy and landscape to that of the first farmers is not as decisive as often stated.

There is a second reason why the transition from hunting to *Neolithic* farming is not easily distinguished in the pollen and landscape record. When the first farmers arrived, probably from across the Pennines and Eden Valley, c3500bc, they too needed to make use of the lightly forested areas and, more importantly, the areas of grassland – exactly those areas which were important to mesolithic communities. Not surprisingly, therefore, the distribution of the earliest farming communities seems to be essentially the same as the mesolithic distribution. And, as far as we can tell, the early farmers supplemented their agricultural production by hunting and fishing, preferring to locate their farms within easy reach of wetland margins. Evidence of such settlements have been found or can be inferred at or near Portinscale, the coastal tarns of Barfield and Ehenside, near Beckermet, and in lowland Furness.

In general the Neolithic is characterised by the first sustained assaults upon the forested landscape. Thus one feature of the Early Neolithic and one sometimes held to mark the arrival of farming is the phenomenon of the 'elm decline', a sudden, marked decrease in the incidence of elm in the pollen record. This has usually been explained by the need of man, in a largely forested landscape, to feed his animals on the leaves of certain trees. Beatrix Potter, for example, recorded that as late as the nineteenth century some Cumbrian farmers might use holly leaves as winter fodder, and bundles of elm leaves tied with withies ready for feeding to cattle have been found on some continental Neolithic sites.

Nevertheless, there are two odd features about the elm decline. Firstly, it seems to have occurred throughout much of North West Europe at approximately the same time: a situation difficult to reconcile with notions of farming being introduced by the slow spread of immigrants. Secondly, trees other than elm were sometimes affected so it

11

is unlikely the broad synchronaeity of the elm decline in Europe can be the result of something like Dutch Elm Disease. The evidence is, however, compatible with existing Mesolithic communities adopting or themselves developing animal husbandry. At Ellerside Moss, near Greenodd, for example, detailed pollen analysis revealed that the first attack upon the forest resulted in oak, elm and lime pollen decreasing by about 20% but that after twenty years elm alone was affected. Such a pattern suggests existing peoples learning for themselves rather than new techniques being introduced to the area.

Whatever the precise explanation it would seem there was a selective utilisation of forest trees for fodder. In some areas the elm and other trees recovered and the utilisation seems to have been temporary and/or cyclical, elsewhere the elm never recovered and semi-permanent clearings seem to have been established. The evidence thus suggests the existence or establishment of settlements within the lowlands, on good quality soils (the existence of which could easily be detected by noting the concentrations of elm) and often within easy reach of the margins of a wetland. In the absence of evidence for cereal cultivation from the earliest sites it is assumed these clearings were pastoral, probably with the animals being folded in them during the winter. The forest beyond would have provided leaf fodder and, in summer, the possibility for the direct browsing of animals. Given that any leaves gathered for winter fodder would have to be transported back to the farm it would seem reasonable to infer an area of managed forest around the settlement with the summer browsing undertaken further away, utilising other areas of elm or natural grassland such as coastal margins or the mountain tops. Theoretically, therefore, we might expect transhumance to have developed early on and for the forest margins to have been pushed back, simultaneously, from the wetland/valley littorals and the high ground. Such a two-fronted assault seems not incompatible with available palaeo-environmental data (the elm decline being dated to 3390+/−120bc at Barfield Tarn and 3150+/−120bc at Blea Tarn in Little Langdale) and the overall distribution of finds and monuments. A concomitant of this form of landscape exploitation would, however, be that a single farming community might, in summer, range widely over an area or between areas and that monuments and sites recorded in spatially distinct localities might have belonged to a single community.

There are two further consequences of such an economic/land use pattern. Firstly, some 'monuments' may have been constructed as a means of demonstrating land ownership (by the inclusion, or not, of ancestral bones) rather than for religious purposes or as a means of giving proper burial to the dead. Secondly, the depletion of the forest as a source of available fodder might necessitate the abandonment of a settlement or lead to the adoption of different farming methods such as cereal cultivation. In the Cumberland lowland there is evidence for both changes: areas of forest clearance around Barfield Tarn apparently being permanently maintained in association with cereal cultivation whilst Ehenside was abandoned after some seven hundred years. The essential point to note is that cereal cultivation does not appear to have been a primary feature of the Neolithic but one introduced about or perhaps after 3000bc.

In the above I have described the kind of landscape exploitation associated with sedentary farming but it is equally possible there was nomadic pastoralism with stock being moved cyclically from one strand of elm to another. Archaeologically and in the palaeo-environmental record such grazing would be almost impossible to distinguish from transhumance related to sedentary farming. The question is, were the elms deep within the forest lopped and the resource managed, or were the animals allowed free browsing? An important consequence of either system would, however, be the eventual depletion of the forest resource, especially in areas of free browsing or in areas of marginal soil and climate. That said, there is no certain evidence for free browsing. Practical requirements would, however, suggest it must have existed and it is worth noting here the shifts in farming and settlement patterns which appear to have occurred, as at Ehenside, at intervals of about seven hundred years, the significance of this timescale being that it corresponds to the length of time when a forest might be killed by undergrazing, with stock preventing tree regeneration by nibbling young shoots. Browsing and undergrazing thus offer an explanation for the apparent ease with which neolithic farmers seem to have cleared large tracks of the previously forested landscape. In passing we might note that an undergrazed (and dying) forest of the kind postulated above would provide parkland landscapes.

Fig 2 summarises the kind of landscape postulated above for the Neolithic, after the adoption of cereal cultivation. Around the permanent farm would be an area of 'inbye land', possibly manured by the stock in winter or left fallow; beyond that would be an area of managed woodland producing leaf fodder, human foodstuffs like apples and hazel nuts, and timber; whilst further away would be areas of seasonal grazing, either natural grassland or browsed, dying, forest where rights might (or might not) be claimed by the establishment of 'monuments'. Once cleared, perhaps after 700 years, this latter area would be available as grassland and potential secondary, if largely pastoral, settlement. As such, the model is compatible with the apparent survival of forest in the valleys alongside farmsteads and the rapid loss of forest on some fell tops, noticeably around the Langdales.

The forest loss was, however, exacerbated by the climatic deterioration thought to have occurred after 2300bc. This was especially noticeable on the high ground of the central Lake District where soil impoverishment, erosion, gullying and associated alluvial fans followed the loss of the tree canopy, overgrazing and the increase in rainfall. At Red Tarn, for example, birch trees began to become entombed in peat c1950bc. Elsewhere, however, the denudation of the landscape was less severe and secondary forest may have survived until relatively recently. Thus the area around Blea Tarn, where the early clearings were abandoned about 2200bc, today supports a remarkable growth of juniper, a plant requiring a mull humus.

Some of the gullies and alluvial cones of nearby Great Langdale may also belong to or be broadly contemporary with this phase of landscape degradation. What is not clear, however, is their relationship to the large-scale production of stone axes which has made its own distinctive contribution to our landscape. The use of volcanic tuff outcropping in the central Lake District for stone axes has been known since the late 1940s but what we still do not know for certain is the appearance of the landscape at that time. Current work does, however, suggest much if not all of the blanket bog on the fell tops is later but the extent of woodland at that time is not clear. Pollen analysis of the valley floor below Rossett Gill in Great Langdale suggests a wooded environment survived there into the Bronze Age and, given the wind direction, it may be this evidence pertains to the valley sides. In all probability the fell tops would have been largely grassland and it is in this area that the extraction of the rock was found to have been by small-scale pits, perhaps the earliest 'workings' and the work of farmers during the period of summer grazing. Such workings are in contrast to the large-scale quarrying which occurred in Langdale and which left a legacy of shallow caves, overhangs and waste tips, the first industrial landscape. One particular area of waste material consists of several overlying tongues of detritus relating to periodic erosion and gullying. The date of this gully erosion and subsequent landscape stabilisation is unknown; it may be Neolithic, it may be later.

Nevertheless, we should assume that during the *Late Neolithic and Early Bronze Age*, from 2200bc onwards, most of the higher ground was largely devoid of trees whilst elsewhere the canopy was thinned or also cleared and such areas thus made available for secondary or more intensive exploitation. It is, therefore, interesting to note how

14

Plate 1 The megalithic circle at Castlerigg, near Keswick, one of the most dramatic prehistoric elements in the Lake District landscape *(W. Rollinson)*

monuments of the period appear to be concentrated on higher ground than in the earlier Neolithic but whether such evidence represents differential survival of evidence, an abandonment of the previously farmed areas or an expansion of agriculture consequent upon an increase in population is not clear. The latter explanation seems the most likely for there is evidence for the expansion of 'clearings' throughout the lowlands about 2000bc and the increased number and size of monuments in this period also suggests an increase in population.

Certainly the Late Neolithic/Early Bronze Age monuments are the most obvious prehistoric elements of our landscape: the great avenue(s) of standing stones at Shap; the stone circles of Castlerigg (Plate 1), Swinside, Elva Plain, Burnmoor and Moor Divock; the henge of King Arthur's Round Table (Plate 2) and the adjacent, embanked enclosure of Mayburgh estimated to contain some 20,000 tons of stone. A number of aspects of these monuments relate to their contemporary landscape. Firstly they hint at the scale of forest clearance. The standing stones at Shap, for example, extend over a mile (2.5km) whilst the monuments on Moor Divock and Burnmoor, admittedly not all of exactly the same date, cover one square mile. Secondly, the circular form of many of the sites reflects the change in house style that occurred during the period; the first farm buildings were probably rectangular, now, and for the remainder of prehistory, they were circular. Thirdly, the monuments employed stone rather than timber

15

Plate 2 The ritual landscape of King Arthur's Round Table and Mayburgh. Originally there were three circles and at least one burial mound here *(Tom Clare)*

reflecting the fact that the farmer was now clearing the land not of trees but of stone. Fourthly, they reflect a social hierarchy reminding us there must have been a network of paths, tracks and trade routes, some of which are probably still in use today.

The existence of a hierarchy is most easily appreciated by comparing size and type of monument, the freestanding stone circles like Castlerigg and Swinside being about 100ft (30m) in diameter whilst the more numerous burial circles, mounds and ring cairns are smaller in size. Sites like Castlerigg were, therefore, the focus for a number of contemporary farming communities each one of which might have its own, lesser circle or burial ground. At the same time, however, the communities which looked towards Castlerigg as their joint focus were part of a still wider grouping whose 'regional' centre would be represented by a complex like Mayburgh and the Round Table. The relevance of this for us is that it implies the landscape would have been divided up between communities, either formally or informally. Equally, the distribution of the various foci tells us something about the location of farming at that time, the existence of Castlerigg, for example, confirming the evidence from Portinscale that the Keswick area, unlike some other parts of the Lake District, has been farmed for some five thousand years. The existence of 'regional centres' in the Eden Valley and Low Furness together with the distribution of contemporary 'finds' shows, however, that the main farming areas must have remained, as in the Early Neolithic, the lowlands around the Lake District massif, with the latter itself probably regarded as somewhat

16

marginal land, a pattern which of course remains today.

How then are we to regard the 'ritual landscapes' like Burnmoor and Moor Divock (Fig 3)? Do these areas with their stone circles, standing stones and burial mounds reflect permanently farmed areas or summer grazing grounds? And were such areas first utilised in the late Neolithic-Early Bronze Age? The answer to these questions must be that at the present time we do not know; the only excavations were nineteenth century ones wholly lacking in environmental analysis. The grouping of cairns and other monument forms in these areas is, how-ever, in contrast to the construction of monuments of similar type but apparently in isolation elsewhere in our area, a contrast which suggests they were regarded or functioned differently. It is, for example, possible the isolated sites served as the focus for an individual farm or kinship group whilst monument complexes like Moor Divock served a number of communities. As foci it would be quite appropriate for them to be on the boundary between groups, betwixt and between. In this connection I was once reminded of how some Cumbrian shepherds' meets were deliberately arranged on a ridge, such as High Street, neither in one valley nor the next. It is, therefore, possible to see areas like Moor Divock and Burnmoor as serving the valleys on either side of the high ground. We might thus expect them to have been used in sum-mer with the gatherings, like the shepherds' meets, at the 'back end'. Interestingly, if not surprisingly in a farming economy, this is the time when the earlier Neolithic foci like the causewayed enclosures of southern Britain appear to have been used.

Fig 3 The ritual landscape of Moor Divock, south-west of Penrith

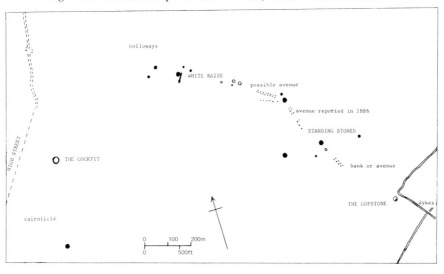

It will, however, be apparent that the introduction of metal items (almost certainly prestigious at first) probably had little impact on the landscape and patterns of farming. Competition from metal axes may, however, have provided a stimulus to the quarrying of the best quality tuff in Great Langdale just as it led to the mining of best quality flint elsewhere. There is, however, no evidence for Bronze Age exploitation of local copper deposits.

Traditionally the Bronze Age is characterised by the appearance of the circular hut but it is probable, as suggested above, that this form of building began to be adopted in the Late Neolithic. By analogy with sites excavated in Northumberland and southern Scotland we might expect hut circles of this period to be unenclosed. One of the best groupings of unenclosed huts within our area occurs south of Shap suggesting exploitation of an area separate from the ritual landscape of standing stones and burial mounds beneath and around the present village. It is, however, by no means certain whether such hut circles were permanently occupied or that they were associated with arable cultivation. The remains of field clearance heaps and banks nearby might indicate former arable plots, the improvement of pasture or later utilisation of the area. Similarly it is by no means certain whether the remains on Tongue How, Kinniside Common, belong to a single period or represent several phases of activity. Nevertheless, they do serve to remind us that elements of the Neolithic landscape were part of the Bronze Age landscape just as they are part of ours. Equally, we should not forget such areas probably still carried some tree cover and that they are, therefore, not true 'Bronze Age landscapes' but 'relict landscapes' of *largely* Bronze Age date.

In a number of areas the hut circles are separated by considerable distances suggesting they functioned differently from those sites where, like Shap, a number of buildings occurred side by side (although not necessarily contemporaneously). The easiest explanation is to regard the isolated hut circles as connected with the use of high pastures and, therefore, probably seasonally occupied – prehistoric shielings. This would explain their relatively small size and poor construction but a concomitant is that they might not be Early Bronze Age but later shielings. It seems safest, therefore, to regard such structures as the remains of prehistoric, rather than Bronze Age, transhumance, a pattern established in the Neolithic and continued into medieval times.

A distinctive landscape usually claimed to be specifically of Bronze Age date is the cairnfield. Essentially a cairnfield consists of numerous, perhaps hundreds, of small mounds or heaps of stones within a rela-

Plate 3 The cairnfield on Thwaites Fell *(Cumbria Sites and Monuments Record)*

Plate 4 The palimpsest of Burnmoor – the ritual landscape of the well known stone circles hardly visible amongst the cairnfield *(Cumbria Sites and Monuments Record)*

tively small area (Plate 3). A further characteristic is that the cairns are often associated with what seem to be the remains of banks (some of which may merely be linear clearance heaps), fields and/or lynchets. Some of the cairns are reported to have produced Bronze Age burials and urns but others yielded no such evidence to early antiquarians and might be considered field clearance. Again, some of the individual mounds have central hollows and might be better described as ring banks. Nineteenth century antiquarians considered them to be the remains of collapsed beehive huts but their diameter is usually too small to accord with such a function. Moreover, when carefully excavated they are found to lack careful construction; the stones seem simply and literally to have been thrown together. An alternative explanation is, therefore, to see some of the heaps – and especially the small diameter, irregularly constructed ring banks – as clearance stones thrown against trees whose decay left a central hollow, just as others might be heaped over or to one side of an earthfast boulder or rock outcrop. We might, therefore, see the mounds recorded in Plate 4 as fossilising a line of vanished trees.

It is also reasonable to see the cairnfields as representing a new phase of land clearance, often on higher ground or valleys floors not previously cleared (like Great Langdale and Mosedale), possibly for arable but equally possibly for pasture. Evidence which might support the idea of associated cultivation is the relatively large volume of soil and burnt stone used in some mounds (the soil, in this theory, being discarded turf, weeds etc). Such mounds have, however, also been claimed to be ritual in character and whilst this possiility should not be excluded, ritual does not necessarily mean 'burial'; rather we should compare the deposits of burnt soil and stones with similar material, deliberately buried in pits, in a Neolithic site at Goodland (N Ireland), apparently as part of a fertility act. Whilst this may be one explanation for some of our evidence it is probable that there was no single purpose for all the features of the cairnfields.

It is equally probable that the intensive land use represented by the cairnfields was not a single event at one moment in time; the cairns and other structures reflect function, a certain type of land use/agricultural practice and not a particular period; not even, necessarily, the prehistoric period. Thus those at Birrel Sike in the Calder Valley *contained* charcoal dated to 1720+/−100 and 1690+/−100bc, those on Burnmoor (Plate 4) have been suggested as belonging to a period c1500bc whilst at Seathwaite Tarn above Dunnerdale the expansion of grassland was dated to 1080+/−140bc. It is, however, necessary to note that both the Burnmoor and Seathwaite dates refer to the pollen

Plate 5 A farmstead and cairns near Lowick *(Cumbria Sites and Monuments Record)*

evidence and not to the structures, it being an (unproven) assumption that the cairns are contemporary with, and neither preceding nor succeeding, the incidence of increased grassland in the palaeobotanical record.

The Burnmoor and Seathwaite dates do, however, suggest the type of land use represented by the cairnfields and unenclosed hut circles was, in some if not all areas, later than that of the ritual landscapes and perhaps more characteristic of the *Middle* rather than the Early *Bronze Age*. As such they might well be contemporary with the expansion of cereal cultivation in the lowlands and the probably not unrelated appearance of formal, rectilinear fields in the Oddendale area east of Shap. Again such a date would explain why a cairnfield seems to overlie the Cockpit circle on Moor Divock (see Fig 3). The possibility thus arises that the Neolithic/Early Bronze Age burial and ritual monuments sometimes recorded in (and hitherto used to date) cairnfields belong to a different period and landscape. Nowhere, perhaps, is this seen more dramatically than on Burnmoor (Plate 4) where the cairnfields swamp the stone circles. There is, therefore, reason to believe that in some localities the cairnfields represent renewed or more intensive exploitation of areas which had been utilised some time before. The cairnfields below Coniston Old Man, for example, might be

21

seen as representing expansion of an earlier grazing ground/clearing represented by the Banniside ring cairn and Bleaberry Haws ring bank and stone circle. Similarly, the cairnfields in the Dunnerdale, Mecklin Park and Gawthwaite areas, on Kinniside Common and on Stockdale Moor might be seen as expansions of areas which earlier generations had established and demonstrated as theirs by the construction of 'burial' monuments.

The type of farmstead contemporary and associated with some cairnfields appears to be that represented at Lowick (Plate 5). Certainly, farmsteads of very similar appearance have been recorded next to cairnfields on Moor Divock and Tongue How, at Waberthwaite, Troutbeck, Brampton and in the Calder Valley. On the other hand there is a second type of settlement to be found apparently associated with cairnfields. That at Threlkeld (Fig 4) is perhaps one of the best preserved landscapes of this type, although others can be seen at Barnscar and on Tongue How. In each of these examples the nucleus is less clearly defined than at Lowick and the buildings tend to merge into yards and small areas of cleared or walled ground beyond which, and approached by a lane, is an unenclosed area with small cairnfield. Clearly the cairnfield here is part of a single, intensive agricultural unit but it is now impossible to tell whether the cairns relate to improved pasture beyond small arable plots or belong to arable fields beyond stock pens. At Barnscar the evidence is in favour of the cairns relating to pasture rather than arable, if only because a significant number are ring banks suggesting, on the basis of the argument presented above, the existence of considerable tree cover and shade not wholly suited to the ripening of cereals.

On lower ground than Barnscar, and possibly at Threlkeld, the pattern was probably one of small arable plots and enclosed pasture/hay adjacent to the farm with unenclosed grazing beyond. Such a system was a very efficient one. By allowing the stock to be folded on the enclosed land in winter those areas were manured at minimal effort, thus maintaining, almost indefinitely, crop yields. The system, of course, is known from later periods and the problem for us is thus to distinguish between prehistoric, Roman and medieval farms, a reminder that there is actually no hard evidence for any of the enclosed farms mentioned above being Bronze Age or indeed prehistoric. Indeed it may be significant that pollen evidence suggests the period of intensive farming associated with cereals occurred in the Barnscar area in the Roman and post-Roman periods. Similarly we might note that the Tongue How example occurs near a 'Lowick type' farmstead suggesting both a different date and form of land usage. There, at

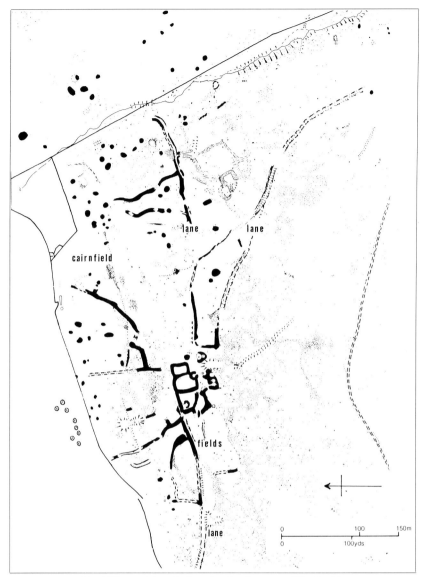

Fig 4 The prehistoric farming landscape at Threlkeld

Barnscar, and in many other places (Plate 6) the relict landscape is best regarded as multiperiod rather than wholly prehistoric.

Reference has been made above to the rectilinear fields near Oddendale just to the east of Shap, but what may be the remnants of similar systems exist south of Shap and in High Furness. In both areas the line of some of the ancient field boundaries – ancient because we cannot be certain they are prehistoric – is continued by existing field boundaries. A similar feature can be observed in the Oddendale–Lyvennet system and has been noted outside Cumbria where there can be little doubt

Plate 6 Hut circles and enclosures at Shap *(Tom Clare)*

the earthworks are of Bronze Age date. It would seem, therefore, that some prehistoric landscape elements other than trackways have survived as functional parts of the present-day landscape. The real importance of such field systems is, however, that they represent markedly different landscapes from those of the cairnfields. A comparison of the two would suggest that the field systems represent a landscape in which there was a reasonable amount of arable whilst the cairnfields represent greater use of pasture. Such a statement should not, however, be taken to mean farming in the prehistoric period was either arable or pastoral, rather that these are techniques and types of land use with most if not all farms being 'mixed' and with access to unenclosed and seasonal grazing. Obviously the proportion of the mix would vary from area to area and the recognition of relatively extensive field systems peripheral to the Lake District massif is again confirmation that such areas were (and remained) the principal and richest farming areas.

The rectilinear field systems of the lowlands might be contrasted again with the linear dyke of Bleaberry Haws west of Torver. In many respects the Bleaberry Haws dyke is similar to the 'ranch-like' boundaries of sites like Plumpton Plain in Wessex, sites which have been demonstrated to be of *Late Bronze Age* date. Whilst this might be the date of the Bleaberry Haws landscape we cannot be certain for such dykes, like clearance cairns, represent a form of land use rather than a specific period. Nevertheless they serve to remind us that there were

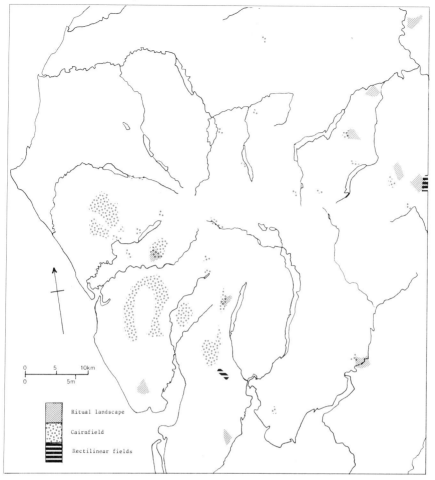

Fig 5 Bronze Age landscapes

prehistoric landscapes of enclosed pasture as well as open grazing grounds.

Linear dykes related apparently to the enclosure of large tracts of pasture/grazing are recorded elsewhere in our area, eg on Moor Divock, possibly associated with a 'Lowick-type' farm. Certainly we must surmise the dykes on Moor Divock to be later than the ritual landscape. Just outside our area, in the Lyvennet Valley, however, similar dykes apear to overlie the rectilinear field systems suggesting a date later than the Middle Bronze Age and a major change in land use. What that change was and when it occurred is, however, not easy to determine but there are hints that in the very *late Bronze and Iron Age* there was a shift to more pastoral farming and a retreat or shrinkage of intensive farming from the higher and/or marginal ground.

This general shift or contraction might be related to the deterioration in climate commencing, perhaps, about 800bc. One consequence

25

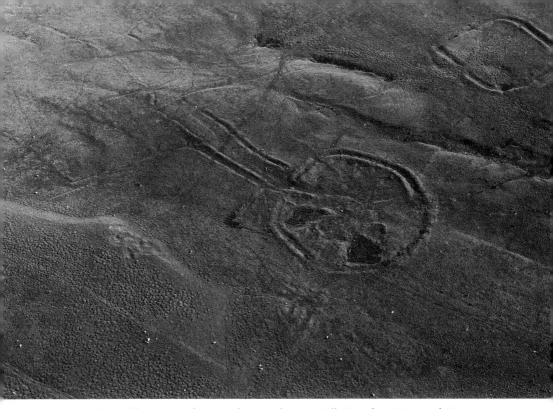

Plate 7 The eastern farmstead at Aughertree Fell *(Cumbria Sites and Monuments Record)*

of this deterioration was the increased height of the water table creating the need, in lowlying areas like the Somerset Levels, for the construction of timber trackways. In our area two such trackways are recorded from the Lyth Valley and, as in the Somerset Levels, we should regard them not as engineered trade routes but as the means to reach traditional grazing grounds, probably established on the wetland margins in the Neolithic.

It is now generally accepted that in southern Britain the Late Bronze Age was associated with major changes in social, religious and technological patterns with the new order being essentially that which the Romans found. Whilst this might also be the case in our area it is less evident, if only because of our lack of dated sites. Nevertheless it would appear that the overall patterns of land use were similar to those previously established, farms in the lowlands and the utilisation of higher and marginal areas for grazing. For that reason we might expect the continued production of clearance cairns and perhaps farmsteads like those of Lowick or Threlkeld; indeed, as suggested above, the latter might well belong to this period. On the other hand farmsteads like those on Aughertree Fell (Plate 7), overlying an earlier landscape of burial mounds, may represent another, late prehistoric, type of settle-

26

ment, one in which a droveway connects the farmyard and unenclosed grazing. This type of farm, however, also appears to be of a kind which survived into the early medieval period and, indeed, is not dissimilar to existing farm arrangements.

The apparent continuity of established land use patterns is underlined by the distribution of the one site type which might be convincingly attributed to the Late Bronze Age/Iron Age period; the hillfort. Our hillforts differ from many in southern England by the simplicity of their construction (there being a single wall or bank) and by their small size. Significantly the largest of our sites, Carrock Fell, is sited, like the others, on ground which in medieval times was used for seasonal grazing. Like others it also overlooks a cairnfield and lowland or valley floor. As such, our recognised hillforts appear to have been deliberately sited to control two types of land use and landscape, not because the two areas were wholly separate but because they functioned together. This pattern (of lowland linked with upland) is that described in later, early medieval Welsh laws and there can be little doubt of its antiquity. Equally, in their control and exploitation of upland pastures the 'hillforts' were not dissimilar – either in function or build – to the 'pound'-like structures on Burnmoor and above Haweswater.

Finally, one might note that there is some evidence, albeit from the edge of our area, for a re-expansion of intensive farming at the very end of the period. In the Rusland Valley, for example, land cleared as late as 736bc, and soon abandoned to the rising water table and sphagnum bog, was again cleared about 13bc.

The Romans, then, found an area which had been farmed for three to four thousand years. Some valleys like Thirlmere still retained extensive tracts of forest but elsewhere, especially in the lowland and some valleys there were farmsteads, fields and lanes, areas of unenclosed common and woodland hedged with legal constraints as in medieval times, a landscape of droveways and established summer grazing grounds, areas used 'time out of mind' by one's forebears. This was the landscape and these the land uses which the Roman military were confronted with.

2
THE ROMAN LANDSCAPE

THERE is a long tradition of treating the Roman period in Britain as a unique event separable from the rest of the history of these islands: there has been a tendency to show it as enjoying no obvious relationship with what preceded or followed it, but rather as a bright light shining between the dimness of Prehistory and the Dark Ages.

There are no doubt many reasons for this view: in the first place, there is our general perception of the Romans and their achievements in political, social, technological, economic and cultural terms. Secondly, the Roman period gains a sense of uniqueness from the fact that it has left a not inconsiderable body of written material – texts, inscriptions and coins. Thirdly, however, the prevailing impression of the Roman period, particularly in the north, has come from *our* preoccupation with sites and landscape – features which were created by the conquerors themselves, such as forts and roads. For a long time this has dimmed awareness of those sites, numerically much larger, which are the evidence of the British during the Roman period – particularly farmsteads, whose archaeological record is more ephemeral. Higham's recent use of the phrase 'the Roman Interlude' helps to redress the balance and stress the continuity of which the Roman period was a part.

It is also necessary to clarify impressions of what the Roman occupation itself actually represented. It did *not* mean the progressive swamping of an indigenous population by conquerors from Italy; Roman administration was always economical of its own manpower. Those who held Britain in the conqueror's name were more likely to have come from the Celtic West than from the Mediterranean. In any case, the long-established Roman custom was to match burdens and privileges, and so in Britain it was a principal aim to create conditions whereby the British themselves might profit from the new situation and assume, as a result, a burden of administrative responsibility. Birth and wealth represented the two chief criteria of success and fitness to undertake responsibility.

A further note of caution needs to be sounded with regard to the state of our knowledge: the very availability of a body of written information has tended to prompt the assumption that we possess a near enough complete picture of Britain from the first to the fifth centuries AD. In the north in particular recent research programmes have demonstrated not only that there are large numbers of native sites to be located, but also that our picture of Roman sites remains incomplete: recent advances in our knowledge of the development of the Roman frontier in the north-west have shown that it is still possible for the state of that knowledge to change fundamentally.

It is also appropriate to regard as incomplete our knowledge of chronologies, topographies and occupation patterns, even of known Roman sites. It is clear, for example, that many military sites incurred complex sequences of successive use and abandonment; the reasons for and consequences of such a phenomenon remain largely elusive, and in the case of some sites we lack even basic chronologies. For example, we are still a long way from achieving a comprehensive picture of Carlisle, the major urban site in the north-west, which must have exercised administrative responsibility over a considerable area. On the other hand, advances have been made through environmental research into human strategies, both before and during the period of Roman occupation. As our knowledge develops of the life style of the native population, so we can progress further towards an understanding of the relationship between victors and vanquished. Such research not only brings greater clarity to our knowledge of the environment, but by so doing provides insights into the political geography which probably greeted the Romans in the north-west and so helps to shed light on the progress of conquest. Thus any writer on the Roman period in the Lake Counties must remain extremely cautious over assumptions and conclusions, regarding both as interim at best.

CONQUEST

The Brigantes are described by Tacitus as the most populous tribe in Britain, and their territory is generally taken to have stretched from the Dee and the Humber in the south to a point north of the Tyne/Solway line; a dedication to the tribe's Romanised tutelary deity has been found as far north as Birrens in Dumfriesshire which may therefore provide an indication of its northern extent. However, we have evidence of other tribal names in the north, of which two, apparently in the west, are the Carvetii (probably centred on Carlisle and the Eden Valley) and the Setantii (perhaps centred on the Fylde, Lancaster and

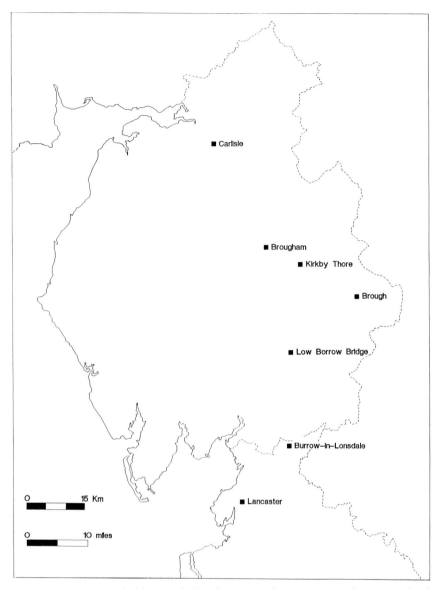

Fig 6 Roman sites probably included in the initial advance into north-west England during Agricola's governorship

the Lower Lune Valley). The existence of such sub-groups, together with the presence of hillforts, suggests that, despite our tendency to blanket the north with a single tribal name, the area must in fact have been split between a number of warlords and landowners who, perhaps, owed a titular allegiance to an overall monarch, who at the time of the Roman conquest of Britain, was Queen Cartimandua.

The physical centre of Cartimandua's power is hard to locate,

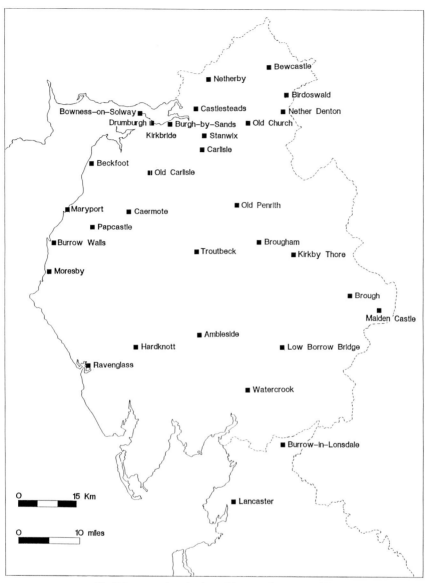

Fig 7 Roman sites in the mid second century AD

though most assume it to have lain east of the Pennines, perhaps indicating that part of her strength rested in control of the good agricultural land of the Vale of York. It is probably reasonable to suppose that west of the Pennines, and particularly in the Lake Counties, people will have been less concerned with the great political issues than with defending their livelihoods against the encroachment of others. Higham has recently emphasised the insularity of the area, and the degradation and under-use of resources which will have led to the need to defend land – and resource – ownership. This insularity of existence in small defended forts or homesteads undoubtedly had implications for the progress of Roman conquest.

From around AD60, Brigantian politics gradually polarised between pro- and anti-Roman groups, and Roman interventions in the north – presumably of a temporary nature – seem to have been required to keep the peace. Although there is no *structural* evidence of this in Lancashire or the Lake District, it is possible that finds of copies of the coins of Claudius in places as far apart as Walton-le-Dale (on the Ribble), Barrow and Carlisle may represent indications of such temporary Roman activity, perhaps in the form of seaborne raids from the Dee which penetrated a short way along river valleys, though leaving the interior untouched. Brigantian stability, however, finally collapsed in AD69; conquest of the north had now become a necessity.

Our understanding of the course of the Roman conquest was for a long time impeded by the predominance of the assumption that the winning of the north was largely the achievement of Agricola, and that the bulk of initial military activity in the area was his. However, Tacitus' account of Agricola's campaign through Brigantian territory in AD79 demonstrates the ease with which Agricola was able to subdue the area in one season, and then turn northwards into Scotland. Agricola was undoubtedly able to take advantage of the obvious disunity which existed west of the Pennines – a phenomenon due in no small measure to the preoccupation of the inhabitants with the problems associated with making a living. We also need to appreciate that Agricola's presence in the north-west was not uniform: in fact, recent studies have served to demonstrate that in all probability Agricola utilised the Lune and Eden Valleys to by-pass the Lake District which, for whatever reason, could evidently be safely left for the moment. Agricola's departure from Britain in AD84 was part of a reappraisal of policy which soon led to a withdrawal of Roman troops first from northern Scotland and subsequently from southern Scotland as well.

Our appreciation of this post-Agricolan period has been much influenced by the general lack of good literary evidence and by Tacitus' clear suggestion that it represented a negative capitulation by Rome. Apart from Tacitus' statement, the only other direct reference to Britain at this time consists of Spartianus' statement that in AD117 'the Britons could no longer be held under Roman control'. The tracing of conquest and consolidation, therefore, between AD84 and 120 has proved to be difficult; only recently has it become clear that, far from a withdrawal, this period saw Roman arms carried into areas like the Lake District which had been by-passed by previous military activity: it also witnessed the rebuilding and sometimes the development of sites which had been established earlier. The period also saw development of the northern frontier, of which the building of Hadrian's Wall represents the culmination.

The Lake District was the type of area in which Roman armies found it diffiult to operate, as can be judged from the long period during which the mountains of north Wales had offered refuge to Rome's enemies. In the present state of our knowledge it is difficult to determine those areas which will have supported heavy opposition to Rome, or which Rome regarded as especially dangerous or desirable. Indeed the solution appears to have been one which would facilitate blanket 'police' coverage.

The encirclement of the Lake District, of which Agricola's route through the Lune and Eden Valleys represents the first stage, was taken further. Sites were established around the coast; Maryport and Kirkbride were in position probably before the end of the first century AD, and over the first two or three decades of the second century they were linked with forts at Beckfoot, Burrow Walls, Moresby and Ravenglass. The establishment of sites on river estuaries represented a well-tested Roman practice, and the river valleys afforded a means of penetration for men and supplies, as well as routes for traders into the interior. Control of these valleys also allowed the Roman army the means to regulate the movement of people and stock between high and low ground according to season. In addition, the coast between Ravenglass and Lancaster may well have had further sites (now lost) located along it.

From such points penetration was achieved by road-building: a route ran west from Carlisle through Red Dial (Old Carlisle) to Maryport, or through Caermote and Papcastle to Burrow Walls and Moresby. From a new fort at Old Penrith, a road ran through Troutbeck (west of Penrith) presumably to Papcastle and Maryport. Although little is known about most of these sites, the complex of structures at Troutbeck suggests that the site may have played a significant part in winning control in the north Lakes. Further south, a route runs from Burrow-in-Lonsdale through Watercrook (Kendal), Waterhead (Ambleside), Hardknott to the coast at Ravenglass. This group of forts has survived sufficiently well for their sites to be appreciated in varying degrees. Watercrook, in the Kent valley, like many Roman forts, enjoyed a river's protection as well as its communication advantages (Plate 8). It was situated in a 'bow' of the river which gave it protection on three sides, though despite this the builders still gave it outside 'cover' of three ditches, a wooden palisade and a stone bank.

33

Plate 8 The Roman fort at Watercrook, south of Kendal. Situated in a meander bend of the River Kent, the fort was protected by water on three sides *(David Shotter)*

Its topography, in fact, provides a good reason for believing that in the Roman period its name was not ALONE (more appropriate to a *Lune* Valley site), but MEDIOBOGDUM ('the fort in the middle of a bow') – the name usually assigned to Hardknott (see note on p48). The presence of the fort in this fertile part of the valley will have minimised the problems of supply: indeed this may have provided the fort with a surplus which could be shared with less fortunate areas.

Similarly situated to take advantage of communications is the fort at Waterhead (Ambleside), which may well have been a receiving, and distributing, point for supplies transported up Lake Windermere – not least iron-ore for processing in the towns (*vici*) associated with most forts. At the head of the Lake this fort was perhaps a major pivot of supplying the interior along the road which led westwards toward Hardknott. The fort at Hardknott enjoys perhaps the most dramatic position of all; with its commanding position looking down on Eskdale, it must have been in a position to keep a watchful eye on the developing agricultural economy of the valley as well as to supervise and check any disturbance which the difficult mountainous terrain might otherwise have camouflaged. Hardknott will have been a cheerless posting, with little or no *vicus* to offer recreational services, and the nearby parade-ground to demonstrate the strictures of discipline required of Roman soldiers (Plates 9 & 10).

Ravenglass is harder to appreciate as a Roman site: such is the cumulative damage done by the sea, by tree plantations, and by the railway. The bath-house, however, represents one of the most substantial surviving Roman buildings in the north-west (Plate 11). The fort's position on a low cliff was intended to protect and supervise port facilities at the mouth of the Esk and to afford protection to a part of the coast less well defended naturally than that to the north of it.

Although such road-routes look feasible on a map, together with others which linked pairs of sites, it would be hazardous to attempt detailed discussion of their roles in the absence of secure dating which, in its turn, will emerge only as a result of large-scale excavation. From relating sites *geographically*, even if we cannot do so *chronologically*, it would appear that in the period c. AD90-130, the Lake District was brought under control through a police network, operated through the *territorium* that was dependent on each fort. However, an appreciation of the strength of such a network would depend on far greater knowledge than we possess of the pattern of use and abandonment of individual sites.

The second century was dominated militarily by frontier construction and reactions to it. The Stanegate, Agricola's road from Corbridge to Carlisle, was, in the late first and early second century, enhanced

Plate 9 The Roman fort at Hardknott, one of the most dramatic in Britain. Perched eyrie-like above the River Esk and overshadowed by the Scafell range, the fort commanded the Roman road between Ambleside and Ravenglass *(W. Rollinson)*

Plate 10 The remains of the *principia*, the headquarter building of the Roman fort at Hardknott *(W. Rollinson)*

by fortification and by the westward extension from Carlisle to Kirkbride. Research at the recently discovered fort south of Burgh-by-Sands has demonstrated that the road first of all had a signalling system which was replaced by forts, and then decommissioned in favour of the new Hadrian's Wall in the early 120s. We have little de-tailed idea of the reasons for the construction of the Wall beyond what can be gathered from Spartianus' statement. It is clear, however, from the evidence of coins and from Hadrian's own visit to Britain that victories had to be won and that the solution was regarded as a prestige project. The Wall and changes of plan seem to indicate that there was felt a need to regulate north-south intercourse in a way that was impossible with the more traditional Stanegate frontier, and that for effective work the soldiers associated with the frontier needed quick and easy access to the frontier zone. Thus by c. AD130 the Stanegate installations had largely been abandoned in favour of the new line.

How deep into the hinterland such trouble spread is difficult to say, though in Cumbria we have no coin hoard evidence of late Trajanic/early Hadrianic times as we do further south in Lancashire. A clearer indication of the vulnerability of Cumbria is provided by the decision to extend the frontier constructions westwards from the terminal fort of Bowness-on-Solway by means of forts, fortlets and watchtowers with linear ditches and palisades around the coast. The extent and pur-pose of these remain open to question though, for once, dating is less problematic; excavation at Biglands, together with epigraphic evidence from Moresby, leaves little doubt that the decision to construct the coastal system coincided with the fort-phase on Hadrian's Wall – that is the mid-120s. Similarly, since the coastal system, like the Wall itself, was apparently decommissioned and recommissioned to dovetail into the phases of occupation and abandonment of the Antonine Wall, it must have related to the military and/or economic threat posed by a lack of control in south-west Scotland.

Space is not presently available to discuss fully the question of the extent of the system, but it should be said that south of Maryport and/or Workington, the coast itself would appear to provide a more effective *natural* defence, and that apart possibly from isolated sites on vulnerable stretches of coast, a coherent system was not extended beyond Maryport or Workington: between Workington and Ravenglass, however, there is some evidence of activity at Harrington and Braystones. Indeed, it is worth bearing in mind that excavation at Ravenglass revealed the presence of a fortlet beneath and thus earlier than the fort itself, which was apparently of mid-Hadrianic date.

Such a comprehensive system of fortification as Hadrian's Wall and the coastal system will obviously have placed a great strain on manpower resources. It would seem, particularly in view of mid-second century abandonment and re-occupations of sites such as Watercrook and Hardknott, that whilst it may have been thought possible to spare troops from the hinterland this, at least in the second century, did not ultimately prove to be feasible.

Such occupation patterns would suggest that locally at least the

Plate 11 The bath-house at Ravenglass, one of the most substantial surviving Roman buildings in the north-west of England (*David Shotter*)

Roman presence stirred some resentment: although there is considerable doubt now over the idea of a Brigantian rebellion in the mid-second century, the evidence of coin-hoards continues to suggest some disturbance in the north-west. A more dramatic indication of at least local disturbance is provided by the tombstone of Flavius Romanus from Ambleside which, with unusual frankness, admits that the soldier was killed by enemy attack *inside* the fort itself. This serves to indicate that Roman garrisons did not have things all their own way.

It is not possible to say a great deal in detail about the occupation of military sites in the third and fourth centuries; evidence is patchy, but sufficient to show that many sites were deserted for periods and that attention was apparently increasingly concentrated on the coast and its immediate hinterland, perhaps indicating that by the mid-third century security problems were more external than internal. It is probably not accidental that this same period apparently saw the handing over of some local self-government to local 'magnates' who must have been sufficiently wealthy to sustain this function. The extent of jurisdiction of the civilian *Civitas Carvetiorum* is not clear. Its very existence, however, demonstrates that even some parts of the north-west succumbed to the allurements of that Romanisation process described by Dio Cassius in the case of German tribesmen – 'The barbarians were adapting themselves to Roman ways, becoming accustomed to hold markets and meeting in peaceful assemblies. They had not, however, forgotten their native ways, their old independence, or their power which had depended on arms. Thus, as long as they were forgetting these customs gradually and under supervision, they were not disturbed by the change in their life and were becoming different without realising it'.

CIVILIANS

Military occupation was never an end in itself: it led both to peaceful conditions which could eventually be left to exist without it and, whilst it was there, gave an impetus to the volume and organisation of economic activity. It is obvious that Romanisation would come about through a combination of supervision and encouragement. The forts effectively provided both through the small towns (*vici*) which grew up outside them. *Vicus* life is not so well understood as fort life, though its potential is clear when we recall the number of major towns in southern Britain which began as extra-mural settlements to Roman forts.

Of Roman towns in the north-west, Carlisle should be regarded as a special case; recent excavations in the Lanes have produced evidence of substantial buildings, including one stone-built house with under-floor heating. Such might be expected of a town which was certainly the administrative centre of the *Civitas Carvetiorum*. However Carlisle, like other towns in the north-west, took its life initially from the military presence.

At present there is no evidence available from north-western *vici* to suggest that they were capable of a sustained life once the military presence had moved on – though again the lack of firm evidence has to be stressed. In general we may assume that the presence of a unit of soldiers in a fort was capable of exercising a supervisory role over *vicus* life, and that the *vicus* population would probably consist partly of people who had travelled with the army, and partly of local people at-tracted by the economic opportunities: for a Roman army unit rep-resented considerable spending power. The money might be spent on locally produced items such as pottery, metalwork, leather goods and jewellery, perhaps sold in local shops or at occasional markets. There would also be a strong official and private market for agricultural pro-duce, as the Vindolanda writing tablets demonstrate. This will have drawn an even wider spread group of local people into the Romanised economic system to service the demand for horticultural and animal food. Finds of animal bones indicate quite clearly the existence of a slaughtering policy which must have involved the local population of the surrounding countryside. Other animals will have been brought in for their hides, for leather – and textile – manufacture probably rep-resented substantial *vicus* business.

Few *vicus* sites in the north-west have been substantially excavated, and Vindolanda (Chesterholm) remains the type site, though it has to be remembered that even there only a relatively small proportion of the site has been sampled. However, some evidence exists for *vicus* growth around at least one exit road at the majority of north-western forts. Indeed, some appear to have been quite extensive: aerial photo-graphy has shown an extensive extra-mural development at Old Carlisle, whilst limited excavations at Ambleside have indicated extra-mural settlement there at a considerable distance from the fort; the heavy agricultural exploitation of the Solway Plain may explain the former, whilst the latter may indicate substantial use made of water transport on Windermere to bring goods into the heart of the Lake District – perhaps indicating the costliness and difficulty of road transport in such an area.

Generally, *vici* developed along one or more of a fort's exit roads, and would grow (and, for that matter, shrink) according to need rather than in obedience to any pre-planned format or extent. This should not, however, be taken to suggest that a *vicus* did not contain important and substantial buildings: the Vindolanda excavations have yielded a bath-house and *mansio* (or official boarding house), and inscriptions from a number of *vici* attest the presence of a wide variety of religious buildings. The bulk of a *vicus* area was probably taken up with the ubiquitous strip-house, built of timber or stone, or a combination of the two. The strip-house represented a domestic and an economic building, for we might expect it to house one or more families, who could make a living by selling produce from a shop on the street frontage of the house, and perhaps manufacture items for sale in sheds or lean-tos situated in a rear yard. Alternatively, we might find industrial activity concentrated into an area, as evidently happened at Manchester and at the extensive site at Wilderspool (Warrington).

Not all items used by a fort and *vicus* will have necessarily been produced locally: apart from the products of itinerant traders (of whom there must have been many) some items will have been the subjects of larger-scale manufacture and transportation. The Roman army certainly had contracts for commonly-used items, such as Samian pottery (coming from Gaul) and the black-burnished cooking pots, which came from southern England. The army itself certainly undertook the manufacture of some pottery and building materials, particularly into the early years of the third century. Legionary manufacturing depots such as Holt (Denbighshire) and probably Walton-le-Dale will have supplied a large market; at a local level, kilns produced these items for a smaller group of sites; Scalesceugh presumably produced for sites such as Carlisle and Old Penrith, whilst Muncaster perhaps performed a similar function for Ravenglass and Hardknott. Undoubtedly other such sites await discovery in the vicinity of Lake District forts. In some places, the civilian population might take a hand in mass production, as almost certainly happened at Wilderspool; this may have represented not only a way of exercising supervision over local tribesmen, but (more positively) the local people's realisation that they could sell their skills through the organised commercial activities which the Romans fostered.

If commercial activity tended to bind Roman and native together, this was no less a function of religion. The Roman and Celtic polytheistic cults enjoyed an obvious affinity, where a similarity of functions allowed two divinities to be worshipped together – often presumably on a site where religious significance had more to do with the local than with the Roman population. Few temple sites or wayside shrines are known for certain, although their presence is often indicated through inscriptions or the discovery of cult objects. Of course, we would expect most attention to be paid to cults which could be described as relevant – the cult of Roman emperors, the chief Roman state deities (Jupiter, Juno and Minerva), gods associated with the army, work or crafts (Mars, the Campestres, Hercules, Vulcan), and Romanised forms of local fertility deities, such as the Lune-god Jalonus, who was worshipped by the retired Roman soldier, Julius Januarius, presumably on the farm which represented his retirement gratuity.

Members of the Roman army and merchants from abroad will also have been responsible for introducing the more exotic religions, most of which had their origins in the eastern Mediterranean: most of these probably offered only occasional interest but some, such as Mithraism, were perhaps more generally current. Of course, the hardiest of such cults was Christianity which is represented by inscriptions at both Maryport and Brougham. With regard to both Mithraism and Christianity evidence is elusive, but sites probably existed in the vicinity of forts particularly when these religions received the active support of the local military hierarchy. Eventually, of course, the attraction of local people to Christianity will have helped to ensure its survival, though little of a *formal* nature is known of Christianity even in the late Roman period.

The presence of the Roman army and its cosmopolitan camp-followers will obviously have introduced many features which the local people would have found strange: for example, wine (of various qualities) began to rival Celtic beer; perhaps also the introduction of bars and clubs in which drinking could take place. The Romans were traditionally great gamblers: finds of gaming boards indicate that this pastime reached the north-west and could therefore have come to involve the local population. Health care, too, will have become available, as is exemplified by an oculist's stamp from Watercrook.

In all, therefore, the forts and *vici* will have presented a view of life very different from that which obtained before the Romans came, though how far local people became directly involved in the changes is open to question.

Whilst the *vici* and other organised complexes may have provided a home and a way of life for some of the local population, particularly those engaged in industry, the bulk will have remained in the countryside, involved in agriculture. A diversifying factor in the countryside, though not one which can be physically located with accuracy, was the soldier who took up farming on his retirement from the army. An example, already mentioned, is Julius Januarius at Lancaster. In general, however, no obvious building-type has been located which could be regarded as diagnostic of such settlement, though a class of more Romanised farm sites has been identified in the Carlisle area, perhaps associated with the Carvetian hierarchy. Some land will also have come under the control of individual fort-units as their *territorium* for growing crops or raising stock – either directly or through leasing arrangements with civilians. The needs of the Roman army for a wide selection of supplies were large: taxation in the form of grain or animals for food and hides will have met a portion of the need, but most will have been acquired by commercial processes, often over considerable distances, since the demands of northern garrisons cannot have been met by the local farmer.

The state of our knowledge of the rural economy has made considerable advances over the last two decades or so: even so, much remains conjectural, and what is generally accepted has to be inferred from a relatively small number of better-known sites. In particular, at lower altitudes, subsequent agricultural activity has done considerable damage to the Romano-British landscape. In the north-west, recent research has gone a long way towards indicating the density of settlement (and presumably prosperity) of areas such as the Solway Plain and the Eden and Lune Valleys (Fig 8).

It has already been observed that the local farmer will have been called upon to yield up agricultural products by way of taxation, but presumably he will either have had, or worked towards achieving, a surplus above this for sale and for his own needs. Environmental characteristics were clearly the chief limiting factors to the farmer's activity: in particular, deforestation and soil erosion will have limited the use to which the higher terrain – that is above approximately 1000ft (305m) – could be put. At the same time the very process of soil erosion from higher levels will have led to enhanced fertility in the valleys.

During the Roman period, deforestation by environmental causes was intensified by the need for timber for building, though in a number of places excavation has revealed that Roman forts were being built in areas already without forest cover, having been given over to grassland or occasionally to ploughing. Deforestation will have affected not only the local farmer's use of the land, but also the materials he used to provide housing for himself. Clearly, stone would have had to be used where timber was in short supply. Thus, for that reason, if for no other, the higher rural settlements would tend to be stone-built – and, incidentally, more resilient to the passage of time.

Rural settlement is identified in generally separate (if not isolated)

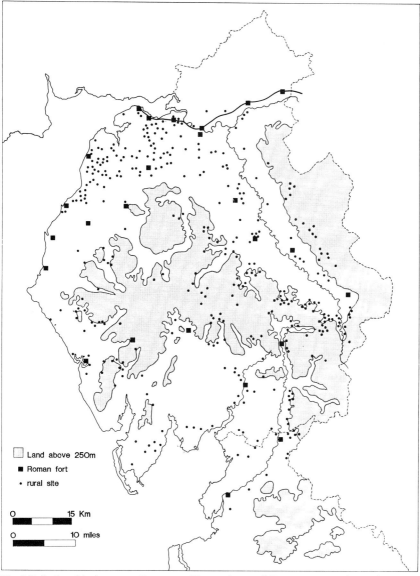

Fig 8 Relationship between Roman military sites and Romano–British rural sites in north-west England

rectilinear or curvilinear forms; these appear to exist contemporaneously, although the rectilinear forms may be more commonly associated with field systems. The majority of sites are enclosed, though some are partly unenclosed, as at Crosby Ravensworth (Plate 12). In general, upland settlements appear at approximately 1000ft (305m), although local conditions may occasionally have permitted or enforced higher or lower limits. Whilst finds of artefacts will permit relatively easy recognition of sites which belong to the Romano-British

43

Plate 12 The Romano–British settlement at Ewe Close, Crosby Ravensworth. The line of a Roman road may be traced immediately outside the remains of the village *(Cambridge University Aerial Photograph)*

period, the paucity of these artefacts usually precludes *close* dating. It is generally held that the more settled conditions which prevailed from the late second/early third centuries provided a major stimulus to settlement expansion, although some sites are undoubtedly earlier than this. Expansion includes not just the appearance of new sites, but also the development of existing ones, as happened at Penrith, where a circular house gave way to rectangular buildings; such a development could suggest the influence of the *vicus* building-types.

The usage of rural sites has again to be generally inferred from the few examples which have been the subject of study. It is self-evident that economic advantage will have lain behind a great deal that was done: the realisation of such advantage might range from the position of a farm close to the Romano-British communications and site net-work to the co-operative management of land which may be visible in the larger field systems. The positioning of many sites tends to indicate that they were intended to take advantage of lower land for arable pur-poses and higher land for stock management. Such arable usage would presumably include the growing of crops for sale and for winter feed for the stock. The smaller fields intended for arable usage were

probably demarcated with low stone banks, whilst larger fields associated with higher turf banks were presumably intended for stock
management.

We can therefore see that in general cereal and hay cultivation took
place in ploughed land in the valleys and the lower slopes, whilst
grazing for animals was provided on the higher slopes, presumably
utilising different areas according to season. It should also be noticed
that land-use was not necessarily static; the Eller Beck complex has
shown arable land given over to pastoral use in the later Roman
period. Some field systems, however, may always have been intended
for pastoralist use, as at Aughertree Fell on the northern slopes of the
Lake District (see page 26), or at Stone Carr (Penrith) where fields were
bounded by deep ditches. Whilst much of the pastoralism was concerned with cattle and the many uses to which they could be put, we
should not forget the role of sheep beyond the provision of food. Finds
of textiles at Vindolanda demonstrate the potential significance of
sheep farming and the local processing of the wool. There is no reason
to suppose that this may not have been carried out by local farmers,
producing amongst other things the rather shapeless garments in
which the 'Cloaked deities' from Housesteads are depicted – possibly
the 'Birrus Britannicus' of Diocletian's Price Edict.

Evidence for organised metal-working in the north-west during the
Roman period is thin: presumably some local craftsmen were involved
in the organised centres like Wilderspool, and we may assume on the
analogy of Manchester that some metal-working was organised
within the *vici*. Indeed the detailed work carried out on the iron-slag
recovered from Manchester suggests that, whilst the source of some of
the iron was local (Cheshire), some may have come from further afield
– for example, Furness. The paucity of evidence, however, makes it
clear that metal-working cannot have constituted a major element in
the economy of the Roman north-west.

Whilst crop-growing and stock-management provided a living for a
large section of the rural community, it should be noticed that for some
hunting must have remained more of a living than a pastime. Areas of
woodland will have provided a habitat for red deer and wild boar,
which could clearly have made an economic contribution.

In short, whilst it has to be said that our knowledge is very selective,
it is becoming possible to see a degree of integration between Roman
and native in the north-west, which exists on the economic, social and
religious levels. The evidence will be seen principally within the urban
context, and in the rural environment in the close vicinity of fort/*vicus*
sites. The wider rural community will have generated what was re-

quired in taxation, and perhaps in some cases, a surplus for sale. However, that the volume of that surplus never reached major proportions in the north-west is clear from the general inability of the *vici* to prosper without active support from a military presence. In this sense, Romanisation in the north-west may have advanced – no doubt more for some than others – but it did not attain the level of urbanisation and wealth-creation that we see further south.

THE LAST YEARS

Traditionally our knowledge of Late Roman Britain is thin, and in the north it has tended to pivot around the 'Conspiracy of the Barbarians' of AD367. As is so often the case, it would appear that we should look less to a single large decisive event than perhaps to a culmination of a longer period of disturbance. Despite the fact that it attracted little respect from ancient writers, it appears that military action in the north by Septimius Severus and Caracalla secured a period of peace during the third century, which was able to survive the internal problems afflicting the western Empire in the middle of the century ('The Independent Empire of the Gauls'). Archaeologically, the effects of neither the peace nor the internal disturbances can be easily pinpointed, although some evidence of rebuilding at Lancaster can be dated to the 260s. Whilst some north-western forts were definitely in use in the earlier third century, the picture is more confused in the later years of that century, though the existence of the *Civitas Carvetiorum* implies a degree of peace, even rather lax military control.

The disturbed political and economic conditions persisted through the third century, culminating in Diocletian's establishment in AD294 of a new form of central government – the Tetrarchy – and the attempted rebellion from it in Britain of Carausius and Allectus. This brought to Britain Constantius Chlorus, one of the tetrarchs and father of Constantine I; although there is no evidence of major enemy attack in the late third century, Constantius was evidently in Britain twice (in AD296 and 305-6); this was a period of rebuilding, and the fort of Birdoswald attests Constantius' involvement in that work. However, some of this work was probably more the rectification of neglect than the repair of war damage.

How far, if at all, north-western tribesmen caused trouble during this period is hard to say, although the activities of scouts/agents (*exploratores/arcani*) suggest that there may have been at least a fear of it. It is evident from the *Notitia Dignitatum* that there was flexibility in military disposition, which perhaps reflects the official realisation that the potential sources of problems were complex. As we have seen, the fate of the *vici* of north-western forts is far from clear, though the evidence from them of reduced activity in the later third and fourth centuries is probably more symptomatic of economic than of security-based problems. There is no direct evidence to suggest the removal of the *vicus* populations into the security of the forts.

There has been insufficient excavation to allow us anything like a full picture of the military occupation in the fourth century. We can, however, be clear that the Lune/Eden corridor will have been maintained – and was in fact enhanced with two structures at Wreay Hall and Barrock Fell – perhaps signal-stations. Occupation clearly continued at Ambleside, and possibly at Watercrook, and it is clear that the military philosophy of the fourth century was to place less reliance on the barrier of Hadrian's Wall itself than on the concept of defence in depth.

Moves in this direction in the fourth century appear to have shifted to the coast. Maybe imperial visits such as those of Constantius Chlorus and of his grandson, Constans (in AD343), helped to shape this policy: certainly the new fort layout at Lancaster has sometimes been associated with Constans. The western sea coast of Britain was now much less concerned with trade than it was with military activities; the construction of bastioned fortifications at Cardiff, Caer Gybi and Lancaster suggests the *possibility* of a coherent west-coast defence strategy, which in Morecambe Bay appears to have centred on the use of a specialist naval unit based at Lancaster. Further north, finds of fourth-century coins in the Barrow area suggest the possibility of a coastal site; more certainly, Ravenglass, Moresby, Maryport and Beckfoot all saw fourth-century occupation, and Burrow Walls, which has produced little except fourth century pottery, may have been a substantially new site of this period. Ravenglass and Bowness-on-Solway (and probably others) saw substantial remodelling even in the later years of the fourth century. It should also be noted that some, though by no means all, of the Hadrianic coastal system between Bowness-on-Solway and Maryport, was returned to commission at this stage, and the milefortlet at Cardurnock may have performed a lookout role.

Therefore, whilst there is no lack of evidence of military commitment on the part of Rome during the fourth century, it must be doubted how far this was protecting a still flourishing economy. The introduction on a large scale of Crambeck wares suggests that the traditional sources of pottery supply in the south were no longer active: a decline in pottery supply no doubt had a consequential effect upon other trade. Indeed, as the century went on, the interest of Rome's dwindling troop numbers was perhaps increasingly concentrated on the coast and the virtual absence of coinage after the early 390s is probably as clear an indication as any that by that time the military involvement was moving inexorably to its end.

As elsewhere, the northern tribesmen must have been thrown increasingly on their own resources; indeed such elements of the Roman army that remained probably disbanded themselves, melting into the local community. Thus, they and the local tribesmen were now forced back into an economy where the major, perhaps sole, economic preoccupation was self-provision. Without the markets and the protection which the army had afforded, there was little else. Without the discipline which Rome had brought, the factional rivalry – no doubt largely over the ownership of resources which had characterised the pre-Roman period – returned to the north-west. The local tribesmen continued to cope with new problems but the 'Roman Interlude' was essentially over.

ROMAN PLACE-NAMES

The identification of the Roman place-names in the north-west has proved extremely difficult: the 'traditional' names, which come largely from identifying *Iter* X of the Antonine Itinerary as a route running from Ravenglass to Whitchurch (Shropshire), can be objected to on grounds of chronological and etymological propriety. In the north-west only two Roman place-names – Luguvallium (Carlisle) and Bremetonnacum (Ribchester) – have any good claim to certainty. We are unlikely to advance very far without the help of new epigraphic discoveries; the paucity of such evidence serves only to emphasise the very small amount of research and excavation that has as yet been put into north-western sites.

It is possible in this vacuum to propose alternative schemes to the traditional place-name arrangements, which solve *some* of the difficulties; the suggestion that Watercrook may be MEDIOBOGDUM rather than ALONE, made earlier in this paper, is one of these.

3
THE DARK AGE LANDSCAPE

For some parts of England the term 'Dark Age' is beginning to become redundant. In recent years advances in fields such as archaeology, place-name research, and the study of Anglo-Saxon charters, have revolutionised our knowledge of the English landscape in the period between the Roman withdrawal and the Norman Conquest. In the process our ideas about many aspects of the evolution of the pre-Conquest landscape such as the origins of nucleated settlement and open field systems have been completely revised. The same cannot be said for the Lake District. Documentary sources relating, even obliquely, to Cumbria before the twelfth century are scanty. Aerial photography and fieldwork have recently revealed a wealth of crop-mark sites in the Cumbrian lowlands, and entire relict landscapes with settlements, fields and boundaries on the moorland fringes of the Lakeland fells. These are thought to relate, in part, to post-Roman times but there has been very little excavation of such sites and firm dating evidence for them is minimal.

Yet the Dark Ages were extremely important in the shaping of the present landscape of the Lake District. Many place-names contain elements derived from Old Norse. Today, Norwegians can often interpret their meaning much more easily than English visitors. Yet despite this widespread evidence of Scandinavian colonisation so far we have no securely-dated settlement site in the area from the Viking period. The Dark Ages in the Lake District are, in this sense, still darker than elsewhere in England. In order to identify surviving features from this period in the modern landscape, and to try and understand how the Lake District landscape evolved between the fifth and twelfth centuries, some careful detective work is necessary in piecing together scattered and fragmentary clues. Although the result of this is still a very incomplete picture, paradoxically this makes the study of Dark Age landscapes in the Lake District all the more fascinating.

THE POLITICAL FRAMEWORK

Before we examine the evidence for the Dark Ages in the Lake District landscape an outline of the political framework within which the area developed between the fifth and twelfth centuries will be useful. The history of the region in the Dark Ages is a very shadowy one but only the main features need be stressed here.

When the Roman garrisons were withdrawn from the north-west in the early fifth century native society seems to have adjusted comparatively easily. There had been major incursions by the Picts in the later fourth century but within a generation of the Roman departure local tribal chiefdoms had been re-established. Sometime during the fifth century these local units merged to form the kingdom of Rheged. Rheged seems to have been centred on the Solway Lowlands, possibly with its capital at Carlisle. Its territory may have extended north into Galloway and its southern limits have been variously set at the Lune gorge, the Ribble and the Mersey. Athough little is known about the Kingdom or its rulers Rheged was a major political force in the north.

The power of Rheged was declining by the later sixth century and in the early seventh century it was absorbed by the expanding Anglian kingdom of Northumbria, perhaps by a dynastic marriage rather than military conquest. For nearly three centuries the Lake District and its surrounding lowlands were under Anglian influence but in the ninth and tenth centuries Northumbria collapsed under the impact of the Danish invasions, leaving a power vacuum in the north-west. This vacuum was partly filled by the British kingdom of Strathclyde which expanded southwards in the early tenth century, pushing its frontier to the River Eamont by 926 along the line that was later to become the boundary between the counties of Cumberland and Westmorland and perhaps extending even further south at times. Although subject to the kings of Strathclyde and later of Scotland, Cumbria seems to have been ruled by its own line of British kings down to 1018. Contemporary with or soon after the expansion of Strathclyde came the settlement of Scandinavians, predominantly Norse, from western areas including Ireland and the Scottish isles. Their colonisation of the Lake District and its fringes may well have been allowed, even encouraged, by the British kings of Cumbria to strengthen the area against English attack.

In 1018 the last Cumbrian king, Owen the Bald, allied himself with Malcolm II of Scotland and was killed in battle against the English. This allowed Malcolm to annex Cumbria which remained part of Scotland until 1032. Cumbria was then in English hands for a few years, first under earl Siward, then earl Tostig, but in 1061 Malcolm III

invaded the north-west probably with the intention of recovering
Cumbria. He seems to have succeeded but at a high cost to the area.
The swathe of destruction cut by his army was probably responsible
for the numerous vills in south Westmorland and north Lancashire
which Domesday Book records as being waste a quarter of a century
later in 1086.

The Normans were slow to bring the north-west under their control
and the northern part of the Lake District may have remained in
Scottish hands for some time after Malcolm's invasion of 1061.
Domesday Book shows that only the Kendal area and the southern
fringes of the Lake District were in Norman hands by 1086. In 1092
William Rufus mounted an expedition which captured Carlisle and
drove out its ruler, Dolfin. Dolfin may have held the area for the
Scottish king or perhaps he was a local ruler who had seized power in
this disputed frontier zone. Rufus had a castle built at Carlisle and
brought colonists in to settle the surrounding countryside. Nevertheless, Carlisle remained an isolated and vulnerable frontier post until
the early twelfth century when Henry I carved up the Lake District into
a series of great baronies whose castles formed a chain of defences
linking south into Lancashire and east to Yorkshire.

MAN'S IMPACT ON THE ENVIRONMENT

In seeking to understand how man shaped the Lake District landscape
during this period we are fortunate in having a more detailed record of
changes in the vegetation cover than for most parts of England. The
Lake District has a wealth of sites at which fossil pollen has been preserved in lake sediments, upland peat bogs and lowland mosses and
the pollen record of successive layers from many such deposits has
been studied to provide a picture of how the vegetation changed over
time. Any dislocation of society which occurred following the departure of the Romans did not disrupt the inhabitants sufficiently to cause
large-scale abandonment of land as this would have been shown by
evidence for woodland regeneration in the pollen record. Instead,
there was a major phase of woodland clearance around the margins of
the Lake District fells which began in Roman times but which may
have reached its peak in many places during the early post-Roman
period. There are indications that a period of warm, dry climate may
have encouraged this phase of settlement expansion and clearance.
Areas which had been cleared of woodland remained open till the end
of the sixth century. This clearance phase has been detected not only in
lowland mosses around Morecambe Bay and in West Cumberland but

also in deposits from upland tarns like Burnmoor Tarn and Devoke Water. Finds of cereal pollen from these tarns indicate that settlement and cultivation spread into the uplands to altitudes of over 900ft (275m) in places, higher than at any time before or since.

The evidence from some upland sites suggests that the surrounding slopes had already been cleared of their tree cover in prehistoric times and that heather moorland rather than woodland was being broken up for cultivation. By this period large areas were already open grassland, moor and peat bog. In places, like the lime-stone plateaus around Shap, exploitation of the environment was so intensive that there may have been no more woodland at this period than there is today. The expansion of settlement in the uplands was, however, accompanied by large-scale soil erosion and the conversion of the thin upland soils to acid podsols. Over-cultivation and probably over-grazing caused a major ecological disaster which permanently altered the landscape in many places, converting large areas into heath and poor grassland. In some particularly sensitive areas, like Shap, the soil was stripped off completely leaving bare limestone pavement adjacent to early Dark Age settlement sites.

Inevitably, this ecological devastation led to the progressive aban-donment of marginal settlements and a retreat into the valleys where the heavier soils were better suited to long-term exploitation. The start of this phase has been dated to around 580 at Devoke Water. The onset of wetter climatic conditions may also have encouraged a down-hill retreat. The Northumbrian take-over of the area is now seen as having been a relatively bloodless one and the sharp fall of population which is hinted at by the renewed spread of woodland at the end of the sixth century is now attributed by some to the effects of a major plague. Certainly some pollen diagrams suggest that in places the abandonment of cultivated land was rapid and extensive, with the spread of scrub followed by the development of a full woodland cover.

From the late sixth century onwards there are indications that the woodland cover was beginning to regenerate in many parts of the Lake District though in some areas soils were so impoverished that trees were no longer able to re-establish themselves. Some minor clearance phases in the lowlands have been linked with the activities of Anglian settlers but at this time the uplands seem to have been largely aban-doned. Although much of the Lakeland fells had been permanently stripped of their tree covers a good deal of woodland probably still remained in the valleys. Renewed woodland clearance, for pasture rather than cultivation, was contemporary with the Scandinavian settlement in the tenth century, and may have been associated with the opening up of the main Lake District valleys for settlement. The troubled period around the time of the Norman Conquest is linked with further regeneration of the woodland cover, followed by signs of a renewed spread of grassland during medieval times associated with the expansion of livestock farming on monastic estates and in the former hunting forests.

EARLY POST-ROMAN TIMES: SETTLEMENT AND LANDSCAPE

The plateaus on the fringes of the Lake District preserve some impressive and fascinating early landscapes. Although these can be identified all round the mountain core the most impressive examples come from the limestone country at the head of the Eden Valley, from Shap eastwards. Most of the countryside below about 800ft (244m), and some of it above this level, has been affected by ploughing in medieval and later times and it is only above this limit that these earlier features have survived on a large scale. The existence of settlements ranging from single homesteads to substantial villages, with their surrounding enclosures, has been known for a long time and, on the basis of a limited amount of early excavation, they have generally been dated to the Roman period (see Chapter 2).

It was once thought that these upland sites were the main areas of settlement for the Romano-British native population whose farming technology was not sophisticated enough to cope with the heavy clay soils of the lowlands. Within the last few years aerial survey has led to the discovery of numerous new settlements in the Eden Valley and the north Cumbrian lowlands. Only in a few places, like the medieval deer parks at Lowther and Brougham, has later cultivation been sufficiently restricted to allow surface traces to survive. These settlements appear to be contemporary with the remains on the fellsides and it is now clear that during the Roman occupation and immediately after the main centres of population were in the lowlands, not the upland fringes. The expansion into the uplands, recorded by the pollen evidence, took place at the margins of settlement on poorer, less attractive land.

As so little excavation of such sites has been undertaken, their continuity into post-Roman times has been assumed, on the basis of the pollen record, rather than directly proved. Nevertheless the probability is that some at least of these features date from the sixth century or even later. In the Crosby Ravensworth area, for example, the remains cover an area of many square kilometres, interrupted in places by gaps due to later ploughing. The settlements, often with the foundations of stone-walled circular huts clearly visible, are surrounded by enclosures and traces of arable fields. Beyond these are areas divided up into larger blocks by stone and earth banks which probably demarcated units of better-quality pasture. These lower pastures are in turn separated from the rough grazings of the open fells by massive earthen boundary dykes, which can be up to a metre high and may have originally been topped by a hedge or palisade. Their purpose seems to have been to keep livestock on the fell grazings in summer from encroaching on the winter pastures and arable land lower down.

The abandonment of these settlements with their fields and pastures appears, from evidence in the landscape itself, to have been progressive and gradual but the actual dates involved are still a matter of guesswork. Desertion of these sites may have started during Roman times as a result of soil erosion but the process was probably a slow one whose chronology varied from place to place. As well as a deteriorating environment a greater desire for security may have encouraged the concentration of settlement into larger communities lower in the valleys. The use of some sites may have continued into the later sixth or seventh centuries but the process had certainly been completed by c1100. An interesting feature of many of these settlements is the occurrence of the foundations of rectangular buildings overlying the main phases of settlement associated with circular huts. Do these represent the last phases of occupation of these sites during the sixth century or are they later in date? It has been suggested, largely on the rectangular layout of the structures, that they may represent a re-colonisation of the fells by Scandinavian livestock farmers in the tenth and eleventh centuries. Equally they could be medieval shielings or post-medieval herdsmen's huts; only excavation would provide an answer.

Although the homes of some of the ordinary inhabitants of this area in the immediate post-Roman period are clearly visible, the locations of the centres of royal power within Rheged are harder to pinpoint. Some of the small pre-Roman hillforts in this area may have continued in use but many estate centres may not have been fortified, making them harder to identify. The strategic importance of the crossing of the Eamont near Penrith suggests that there ought to have been a centre here and one has been tentatively identified near Clifton. A stray documentary reference has been interpreted as referring to a royal centre somewhere in the Lyvennet valley east of Shap and a likely site for it has been identified in a large polygonal enclosure with traces of buildings inside, just to the west of Crosby Ravensworth.

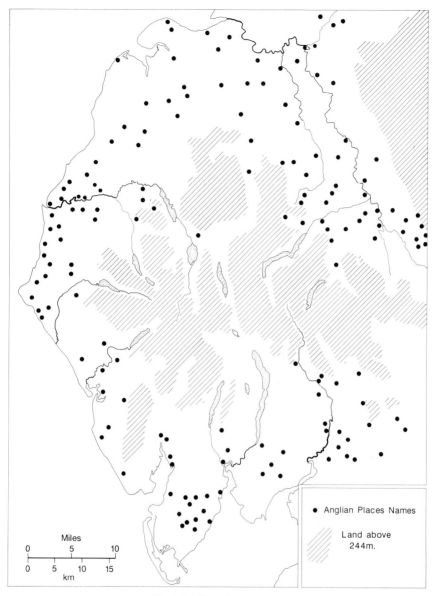

Fig 9 Anglian place-names

THE ANGLIAN SETTLEMENT

The absorption of Cumbria by the kingdom of Northumbria in the early seventh century tends to be viewed now as a peaceful takeover rather than the military conquest and mass genocide which was once the favourite scenario. It is believed that Northumbrians probably took over the major estates without much displacement of the existing population. The spread of early Anglian place-names around the Lake

District is fairly thin (Fig 9) suggesting that while there was some influx of settlers and peasant colonisation – perhaps to an area whose population had been cut by epidemic rather than war – the area was not swamped by incomers. Place-names containing the elements -ham (a homestead: Askham), -ceaster (an ancient fortification: Muncaster), -tun and -ington (a homestead or village: Irton, Irthington), and -wic (a village or dairy farm: Butterwick) probably date from before 900. They are scattered fairly evenly through the Cumbrian lowlands but are almost absent from the mountain core (Fig 9). This has been interpreted in the past as an indication that the Anglian settlers had an arable-oriented farming system and tended to shun the uplands. Certainly the scarcity of Anglian names containing woodland clearing elements suggests that they broke little new ground. On the other hand, if there was a major cut in population during the sixth century then there may have been plenty of room for new colonists within the lowlands and no need for incomers to push into the fells.

Despite the abundance of Anglian place-names there is a conspicuous dearth of evidence in the landscape for their presence, if one excepts religious sites. Excavation has only produced one non-ecclesiastical settlement site which dates from the period of Northumbrian influence; beside Bryant's Gill, a small stream at the head of the Kentmere valley, close to some of the highest areas of the eastern Lakeland fells, a rectangular building 10m long and 5m wide with a central strip of paving has been excavated. Charcoal from within the building gave a radiocarbon date of AD700+/−80; and there are close parallels between this and other upland farmstead sites of similar period at Ribbleshead and in Teesdale. The date of occupation is too early for the supposed Scandinavian penetration of the wooded dales. Whether occupied by native Briton under Northumbrian rule or Anglian colonist, the farmstead shows that at least one of the valleys close to the heart of the Lake District was inhabited at an earlier period than has usually been accepted.

(opposite) The Castlerigg Stone Circle, near Keswick, is thought to date from the late Neolithic – early Bronze Age period *(Simon Crouch)*. *(over page)* Created by Manchester Corporation in 1894, Thirlmere was the first of the great reservoirs within the Lake District *(Norman Duerden)*

VIKINGS AND CUMBRIANS

The southward expansion of the Kingdom of Strathclyde into the Lake District in the early tenth century is marked by the occurrence of Brythonic place-names over an area extending from the Solway Firth south to a line roughly from the River Derwent to the River Eamont (Fig 10). The old county name 'Cumberland' itself derives from this phase of settlement, as does Penrith, and places whose names incorporate the element 'caer' ('fort', 'defended settlement' or perhaps sometimes merely 'farm') as in Carlisle. Some places with Brythonic names like Dunmallard Hill near Ullswater have remains of defensive enclosures which may relate to the British colonists but so far none of them have been excavated. Many places with Brythonic names became centres of parishes and townships and were clearly of some importance. Penrith itself is likely to have been the centre of a large estate. On the other hand some places with these names in the Eden Valley are on more marginal sites suggesting that the colonists moved into unoccupied areas between existing settlements. The occurrence of Brythonic names like Carrock Fell among the mountains of northern Lakeland may indicate an expansion into the uplands, possibly with the use of shieling systems, which may have been roughly contemporary with the Norse penetration of the Lake District dales.

The nature of the Scandinavian settlement in the Lake District has been debated. Was it a large-scale colonisation or merely isolated bands of refugees moving into unoccupied areas? Was it a full-scale military conquest or an aristocratic takeover by a few powerful people which left the existing pattern of estates and settlements largely intact? Although it has been suggested that the incomers were principally livestock farmers and, unlike the Anglian colonists, deliberately sought out upland pastoral areas rather than lowland arable ones, there are many reasons for suggesting that the main power-centres of the Scandinavians were in the lowlands. The distribution of parishes and townships whose names contain Norse elements, and the scatter of Viking-period crosses, both of which highlight the estate and administrative centres, are concentrated in three areas within which Scandinavian settlement was particularly dense. These were the west

(opposite above) Sheep have long been important in the development of the Lake District landscape. Here at Kentmere Hall, a 14th century pele tower built as a refuge against marauding Scots, Swaledales are gathered for dipping *(Norman Duerden)*. *(opposite)* Townend, Troutbeck, is a fine example of a wealthy yeoman farmer's house. Built around 1626 by George Browne *(Norman Duerden)*

61

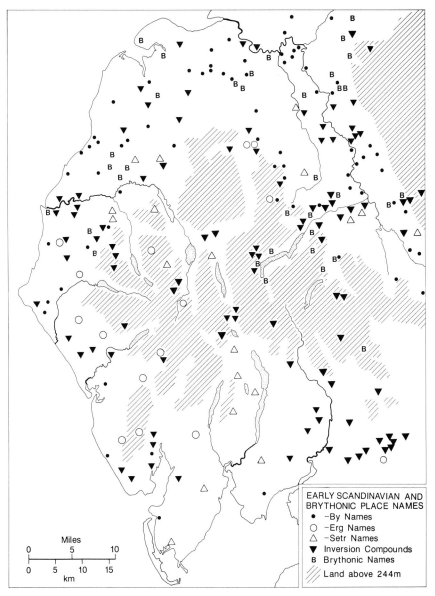

Fig 10 Early Scandinavian and Brythonic place-names

Cumbrian lowlands, south Cumbria, particularly the Kent Valley, and the central Eden Valley around Appleby.

Norse-derived place-names are less frequent in the Solway Lowlands (Fig 10). This is the area in which the distribution of Brythonic place-names suggests that the influence of Strathclyde was strongest. Here Norse-derived names tend to be attached to places with a fairly low status, not parish or township centres, suggesting that the Britons restricted Scandinavian settlement, allowing isolated incomers to take some unoccupied sites but not permitting immigration en masse. It is likely that Scandinavian settlement in west Cumberland and the Appleby area was actively encouraged by the Cumbrian rulers anxious to obtain Norse support against the English. The close association between areas with many Scandinavian place-names and former monastic sites like Heversham, Dacre, Beckermet, Brigham and Workington may indicate that the collapse of the church in these areas provided estates which could be transferred to Viking leaders. The fact that the major territorial divisions of west Cumbria: Allerdale, Copeland, Furness, all have Norse names suggests that they were able to take over the main estate centres. Moreover, the name Copeland, literally 'bought land', suggests that some of the incomers may have acquired their lands by purchase rather than conquest.

It is now thought that the Scandinavian settlement may have involved three contemporary and complementary processes. The first was the takeover of existing settlements, particularly estate centres, in those parts of west Cumbria and the Eden Valley where many parishes and townships have Norse-derived names. At the same time there was an infiltration of other lowland areas by Norse colonists who often seem to have established themselves on more marginal sites between existing settlements. Thirdly there was the colonisation of the upland valleys and wastes, whether by incomers who could not establish themselves elsewhere or by migrants from the nearby lowlands in search of fresh pastures.

Place-names incorporating the Norse element -by (a farmstead) may indicate a fairly early phase of Norse settlement. They tend to occur around the fringes of the Lake District rather than in the upland dales and many places with -by names in west Cumbria and north Westmorland are parish centres on the best soils. A later stage in the colonisation process may be marked by names ending in '-thwaite', from the Old Norse word for a clearing, possibly from woodland or waste. Many such names can be found in the valleys, perhaps tying in with the phase of clearance identified in the pollen record. Some of these secondary clearance names need to be treated with caution. It is not clear when Norse speech died out in the Lake District. The use of Scandinavian-type runes at Carlisle, Pennington and possibly Bridekirk suggests a form of Scandinavian 'writing' survived into early medieval times but despite this some authorities believe that the Norse language went out of use fairly quickly. Even if this was the case words like 'thwaite' may have entered the local dialect and remained current long after the initial Norse settlement. Some settlements whose names have -thwaite endings are prefixed by personal names which must post-date the Norman Conquest. Within the fells many names of topographical features appear to derive from Old Norse. However, terms like 'beck' (stream), 'dale' (valley), 'fell' (hill or mountain) and 'gill' (ravine), entered the local dialect and are still used by Cumbrians today so that some of these names may have been coined centuries after the Norse settlement. Nevertheless, the lack of Anglian place-names among the central fells and the presence of names incorporating Norse elements of types which are known to be early suggest that colonisation of the dales was contemporary with Scandinavian settlement in the surrounding lowlands.

Between the ninth century and the Norman Conquest there are indications of a build-up of population and an expansion of settlement in the lowlands around the Lake District. A general rise in the native population independent of the impact of the incoming Norse may have led to the colonisation of the uplands but the Scandinavians nevertheless gave this movement a distinctive character. The Norse pastoral farming system had involved the use of 'saeters', summer grazings high in the mountains to which animals, especially cattle, were sent along with part of the community for a period of several weeks to make the most of the high pastures, and to take the pressure off grazing areas closer to the main settlement. These summer grazings and temporary huts which were built close to them were given particular types of name. One was 'saetr', still current in modern Norwegian, producing modern place-names which often end in -set or -side: (Swineset, Ambleside). The Scandinavians also introduced another word 'aergi' for a shieling which had been borrowed from Ireland or possibly western Scotland. Modern place-names incorporating this word often end in -er or -ergh (Winder, Sizergh) (Fig 10). Aergi names seem to have been used at an early stage of Norse colonisation and then to have fallen out of use as they occur mainly in lowland or semi-lowland areas such as the Kent Valley and west Cumbria and hardly ever in the uplands. Saeter names, while they also occur in the fringing lowlands, are more common among the lower fells and main valleys of the Lake District. A third word, 'skali', was also used to denote shieling sites giving rise to places whose names contain 'scale'. These names often occupy the highest, most remote sites of all.

Overall the distribution of these names suggest an evolutionary sequence with first aergi and then saetr going out of general use leaving skali as the name which was generally used for shielings in medieval and later times. Linked to this was the steady push of permanent settlement into the mountains by the permanent colonisation of what had once been temporary shieling sites. Shielings were generally located

Plate 13 Sadgill, Long Sleddale, a former shieling site now occupied by a permanent farmstead *(Ian Whyte)*

close to a stream for watering livestock and the areas around them were often used to produce crops of natural hay for fodder. Under pressure of population such sites were ideal for conversion into permanent farmsteads, with new shieling sites being established higher into the mountains (Plate 13). The very fact that so many modern farms bear names containing shieling elements shows how widespread this process must have been. Colonisation continued from the tenth century to at least the fourteenth. It is probably because of this conversion from shieling to farmstead that so few shieling sites have been discovered in the Lake District. Most of the ones which are known are high in the mountains and are likely to be much later than the pre-Conquest period.

Despite the abundance of Scandinavian place-names, so far not a single settlement site securely dated to the period of Norse colonisation has been identified. It can be plausibly suggested that this is largely because sites first colonised during the Viking age have remained in constant occupation ever since. However, in many parts of the Lake District above the level of later improved land one can come across the foundations of rectangular stone buildings which might be sixteenth-century squatter homesteads, medieval shielings – or just possibly Viking-period farmsteads.

Plate 14 The terraced mound behind Fell Foot farm in Little Langdale may be a Viking-period 'thingmount' *(W. Rollinson)*

Although there are so few tangible traces of settlement from the Viking period in this region one curious site is worth mentioning. In Little Langdale, close to the very hub of the Lake District, stands the farm of Fell Foot. Clearly visible from the summit of the rocky knob of Castle Howe immediately to the north, is a squarish mound, its sides now badly worn. A few years ago, before it was damaged by the passage of farm vehicles, the edges of the mound were more clearly cut into a series of terraces (Plate 14). The shape of the mound closely resembles Viking-period thingmounts or assembly places elsewhere in Northern Europe, the nearest parallel being in the Isle of Man. Place-name evidence suggests that another such site once existed near Shap. However, the earthwork at Fell Foot, so near the heart of Lakeland and close to the Roman Road over the Hardknott and Wrynose passes linking Langdale with Eskdale, would have made an ideal assembly place for people from throughout Cumbria. Was this site really a Viking thingmount? The answer is by now a familiar one; without excavation it is impossible to be certain from its shape alone.

THE EARLY-CHRISTIAN CHURCH AND THE LANDSCAPE

We know virtually nothing about the Christian church in the Lake District in the period between the end of Roman rule and the Northumbrian takeover. The suggestion that Carlisle remained a diocesan centre in post-Roman times is pure guesswork although, if this was the administrative centre of Rheged, it would have been the most likely place for such a survival. The lack of evidence for Christianity at this period might be taken as indicating that there were few Christians around, or, alternatively, the lack of identifiable early church sites may show that they are mostly still in use.

Some church dedications are thought to indicate early ecclesiastical sites. The fifth-century Cumbrian saint St Ninian is commemorated in the name Ninekirks attached to the parish church at Brougham although the church is actually dedicated to the Saxon St Wilfrid (Fig 11). Ninekirks is the most likely candidate for an early Celtic monastic site in this area. The church stands in a remote site beside the River Eamont and on the opposite bank are a series of caves which could have been used as hermits' cells. Some pre-medieval burials have been discovered below the chancel of the present church and a hoard of Roman coins found in the churchyard indicates even earlier activity on the site. Immediately to the east of the church aerial photography has picked out an oval enclosure with traces of structures inside. The form of this suggests parallels with Dark Age Irish monastic enclosures.

Another early saint associated with the Lake District is St Kentigern, or Mungo. His twelfth-century biographer describes Kentigern as having undertaken a mission to convert the heathens living in this remote mountain area. The biographer's statement that Kentigern set up a cross at a place named Crosfeld, possibly Crosthwaite near Keswick, whose medieval church is dedicated to St Kentigern, is probably an invention. Nevertheless, eight churches in the northern part of the Lake District are dedicated to the saint (Fig 11). Many of these dedications cannot be traced back beyond the Reformation but this is largely due to inadequate documentation. It is doubtful if they originated as early as Kentigern's own lifetime but it is quite possible that they date from the tenth-century expansion of Strathclyde into north Cumbria, the Strathclyde Britons perhaps introducing the cult of Kentigern who was, after all, their own local saint.

If church dedications are rather suspect indicators of early church sites then holy wells are even more dubious. They are found throughout the area, often in close association with a church or a chapel but sometimes completely on their own. On the hillside above the churchyard at Gosforth is a holy well enclosed by the foundations of a medieval chapel. The well itself may be much earlier. Many wells have vanished and are only recorded on early Ordnance Survey maps or in local tradition but some can still be seen. Where they stand close to a

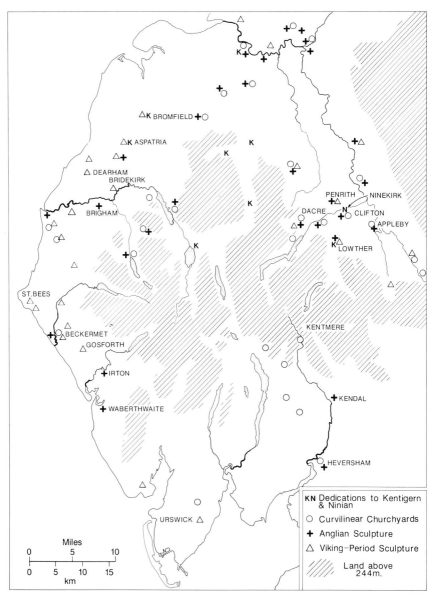

Fig 11 Curvilinear churchyards, Anglian and Viking-period sculpture

church and bear the same saint's name as the church's dedication this may simply have been transferred to the well. Wells tend to be associated with a good deal of folklore but very little fact. Holy or magic wells were certainly associated with many early-Christian saints or with churches dedicated to them but this does not necessarily prove that a well dedicated to St Ninian was used during the fifth century. The veneration of wells and springs went back to pre-Christian times and it is likely that, in the Lake District as elsewhere, many pagan wells were converted to Christian use and that this in turn may have influenced the siting of later churches.

Very few Cumbrian churches have any surviving stonework dating from before the Conquest although it is probable that many medieval parish churches in this area are built on, and in some cases partly from, the remains of pre-Norman ones. The most complete building is the church at Morland, south of Penrith. The tower, dating from the tenth century, with its narrow, round-headed windows, is the best example of Anglo-Saxon architecture in the north-west.

It is the churchyard rather than the church which often provides clues to the early-Christian origins of sites in the Lake District. Most churchyards which were established in medieval times and after are square or rectangular in plan but early-Christian churchyards were characterstically circular or oval (Fig 11). The existence of a curvilinear churchyard does not automatically denote an early site. The one at Troutbeck, where there is no evidence of a church before the sixteenth century, and the example at Ambleside, which did not acquire the right of burial until the seventeenth century, are both dubious candidates for early-Christian status. Nevertheless, the existence of curvilinear churchyard boundaries is a prompt to look for other evidence of ancient origins. Many Lake District churchyards were distinctly curvilinear in the nineteenth century, as can be seen from early Ordnance Survey maps, but have since been altered and extended. Good examples still survive at Barton and Clifton near Penrith, at Kentmere, and at Crosthwaite, near Kendal. At Dacre the break of slope marking the old curving churchyard boundary is visible to the south of the church within the subsequently extended church-yard. The pattern of roads around a church sometimes fossilises a curving boundary though, as at Heversham and Loweswater.

During the 300 years of Northumbrian control in the Lake District the Christian church seems to have become more developed and organised. A number of Anglian monastic sites can be identified. Those at Dacre and Heversham are recorded in documentary sources. At Heversham there are reports of foundations of buildings which may have been associated with the monastery being discovered in the churchyard. Recent excavations at Dacre have uncovered evidence of the earlier monastery. To the north of the church within a larger oval enclosure remains of pre-Norman timber buildings were discovered. These may have been secular in function and the actual monastic buildings are likely to underlie the medieval church and churchyard (which may have used part of the monastic enclosure as its boundary on the south side). Excavation showed that the boundary of the churchyard to the north was redefined around 1200 with the construction of a massive boundary wall which truncated the earlier monastic precincts. The wall, and the chancel of the present church which was also built around 1200, contain quantities of worked red sandstone derived from an earlier church or perhaps even the monastery referred to by Bede.

Other Anglian monastic sites can be identified by the survival of sculptured stones, principally crosses. Anglo-Saxon sculpture was closely associated with monasteries and does not seem to have been produced for secular patrons unlike Viking-age sculpture. Twenty-five items of sculpture from 15 sites have been discovered in and around the Lake District (Fig 11). Most of these were crosses, probably erected as memorials to the dead or to saints rather than as individual grave markers. The most complete example, still in its original position, is at Irton, north of Ravenglass (Plate 16). At Beckermet, a few kilometres further north, the shaft of another cross still stands in situ. Elsewhere such crosses usually survive only as fragments of the shaft or head.

Plate 15 The late tenth century tower of Morland Church, near Penrith, is the finest example of Anglo-Saxon architecture in the north-west of England *(Ian Whyte)*

Plate 16 The Anglo-Saxon sculptured cross at Irton, north of Ravenglass, one of the most complete examples in Cumbria *(Ian Whyte)*

They have virtually all been found at or near churches. One advantage of stone sculpture over other types of pre-Conquest art, metalwork or illuminated gospels for instance, is that it is not readily portable and most of the pieces which have been discovered have probably not moved far from their original sites. Often these fragments have been discovered in the actual fabric of churches during nineteenth-century rebuilding. In many cases the remains of the crosses have been brought inside the church for safekeeping.

The advent of the Vikings as raiders and settlers is likely to have disrupted the Anglian church considerably. Many monastic sites were located close to navigable water making them particularly vulnerable to seaborne raiders. A documentary reference from the early tenth century records the abbot of Heversham in flight from raiders and it is probably significant that the two sites in the Kent valley, Heversham and Kendal, which have Anglian sculpture do not have any from the tenth century, suggesting that the organisation of the church in this area was totally shattered.

The Scandinavians may have arrived in the Lake District as pagans but they were rapidly converted to Christianity. Perhaps the most attractive features to survive from the Dark Ages in this region, and certainly the most numerous, are items of Viking-period sculpture. Such sculpture is much more widely distributed than Anglian crosses: at least 36 sites and 115 items are involved. This has been interpreted as reflecting a change in patronage. Anglian sculpture is believed to have been produced solely for monastic communities and even then not in great quantities. Viking-period religious sculpture may have been commissioned by a wider range of secular patrons as status symbols. While Anglian crosses probably indicate the sites of former monasteries Viking-period sculptured stones are likely to reflect foci of lay power such as estate centres. The distribution, with concentrations in the lowlands of West Cumberland, the central Eden Valley and the Kent Valley, matches closely that of parishes and townships bearing Scandinavian names.

Despite the disruptions which the Norse settlement is likely to have caused there is a strong continuity between Anglian and Viking-period sculpture. The Scandinavian incomers did not have a tradition of carving in stone so they adopted motifs and styles as well as techniques from Anglian sculptors. They added their own characteristic styles of ornament and design though; the wheel-head cross which is the characteristic form of Viking-period cross seems to have been derived from Ireland while many aspects of decoration appear to have been derived from Scandinavia. Anglian crosses have great uniformity of

71

style over wide areas stressing that the scattered monasteries were in close contact with each other. Viking-period sculpture has more distinctive local and regional variations highlighting the work of different groups of sculptors and stressing the political fragmentation of this area in the tenth and early eleventh centuries.

The Viking-period cross at Gosforth, still standing on its original base to the south of the parish church, is the most complete example, a major artistic achievement and at the same time an enigma (Plate 17). It is a Christian symbol with a Crucifixion scene on the east face. This is the only undoubtedly Christian carving on the monument though; other faces show scenes derived from Norse mythology while the lower part of the cross shaft is carved in a scale pattern which may represent Yggdrasil the tree in Norse legend which supported the world. Was the patron who commissioned the work hedging his bets? Or, less cynically, was the sculptor exploring some of the parallels between Christian teaching and Norse mythology? Admittedly, it is not always easy to interpret the motifs; 'pagan' sculptures may in some cases be Christian ones seen through Norse eyes. The Crucifixion scene on the Gosforth cross shows a woman below the cross – presumably Mary Magdalene – but the style in which she is carved is pure Scandinavian. The 'fishing stone' inside the church also has clear links with carvings in Denmark and Sweden.

As well as crosses, Viking-period sculptors also produced hogback stones. These appear to have been adapted from Anglian stone shrines, possibly as funerary monuments to local leaders, and have no direct parallels in Scandinavia. They are carved to represent contemporary houses with a curved ridge line and sculptured tiles on the roof, eaves and curving walls. Some of them, like the Warrior's Stone in the church at Gosforth, have carving of battle scenes. Good groups of hogbacks are preserved in the churches of Dearham and Lowther, while outside the parish church in the centre of Penrith is the 'Giant's Grave', a group of four hogbacks and two cross shafts (Plate 18).

The antiquity of territorial units in the Lake District has already been stressed and early parishes were created within this framework of land ownership. An ecclesiastical division of the Lake District and its surroundings is likely to have taken place during the period of Northumbrian rule. If the number of curvilinear churchyards and churches with Anglian sculpture has any significance the region must have been quite carefully parcelled out between various churches and monasteries and the origins of the medieval parochial system probably date from this time. The Scandinavian settlement may have caused disruption but the system appears to have weathered this. Indeed the appearance

Plate 17 The east face of the Gosforth Cross showing the Crucifixion. The cross marks a major artistic achievement of the Viking period and combines Christian dogma and Norse pagan mythology *(Ian Whyte)*

Plate 18 The Giant's Grave, Penrith, a group of two cross shafts and four Viking-period 'hogback' tombstones *(Ian Whyte)*

of Viking-period sculpture at sites without any evidence of earlier ecclesiastical origins may indicate that the parochial system was being extended during the tenth century, perhaps as a result of population growth.

THE COMING OF THE NORMANS

The Norman annexation of Cumbria and their establishment of a ring of great estates around the Lake District emphasises the important element of continuity in the landscape between Dark Age and medieval times. Most of the great baronies into which the medieval Cumbria was divided were based on existing territorial units. These usually incorporated an area of arable lowland, within which the estate centre was located, and a slice of upland grazing. These economic units often coincided with, and indeed had given rise to, early parishes whose mother churches served their vast territories. The boundaries of these ancient estates followed topographical features forming natural units of great durability in the landscape. The Norman motte and bailey castles and their later planned towns were sited at or close to the pre-existing estate centres, often marked by ancient ecclesiastical sites. Thus the Norman castle and borough of Cockermouth is located near the early ecclesiastical centre of Brigham with its Anglian and Viking-age sculpture, while Egremont Castle and town are only a short way from the early monastic centre of St Bees. The motte of the earliest castle at Kendal, and the medieval borough below it, are immediately adjacent to the church which served the huge medieval parish of Kendal, and which probably stands on or close to the site of an Anglian monastery. On a smaller scale, the parish of Crosby Ravensworth east of Shap is such an obvious natural unit with its limited area of arable land low down in the valley, its improved grazings on the lower fells and its hill pasture above that it is difficult not to believe that here is a block of territory whose boundaries as medieval manor, parish, and pre-Conquest estate may go back to Roman times or even earlier. Such suggestions are impossible to prove although analogy with better-recorded and more intensively studied areas further south makes it quite likely. If this is so then the framework of estate and parish within which the landscape of medieval Lakeland was organised had probably been inherited from before the Conquest.

THE DARK AGES AND THE MODERN LAKE DISTRICT LANDSCAPE

This chapter has highlighted just how little we know about the Dark Ages in the Lake District and their effect upon the landscape. Tangible elements from this period are scarce in the present landscape and the lack of dating evidence compounds the problem. Of the features which are fairly securely dated the most fascinating and evocative must surely be the Anglian and Viking-age sculpture, along with the landscapes of settlements, fields and dykes dating from Roman and immediately post-Roman times which one can walk through on some of the outlying fells. Much of the rest of the story is obscure. It is probable that there are a good many more features in the modern landscape which relate to the Dark Ages than is generally realised. The problem, which has become a refrain throughout this chapter, is that we do not have the dating evidence. This has largely been the result of the comparatively limited amount of excavation which has been undertaken in the Lake District, and the bias of much archaeological work towards pre-historic and Roman sites rather than those from the Dark Age and medieval periods. Given the paucity of early documents – and the limitations which this also imposes upon the study of place- names – it is to archaeology that we must look for more detail to fill out the picture and for more secure dating evidence.

There may also be more subtle legacies from the Dark Ages in the modern Lake District landscape. It has already been suggested that many of the limestone pavements on the outlying fells are man-made deserts which date at least in part from this period, while much of the final clearance of woodland and the creation of the bare grassy and heathy hillsides which are so familiar today were the work of Dark Age Britons and Norse colonists. The familiar Herdwick sheep which symbolises the farming economy of the high fells may have been introduced by the Norse – although it has no direct parallels in Scandinavia and some people believe that the breed goes back to prehistoric times.

The territorial continuity from Dark Age to medieval times has already been stressed, the pattern of estates and parishes from this period providing the framework within which later settlement developed. The siting of much of the rural settlement in the area and most of the parish churches goes back to this period even if the structures which occupy the sites today are much more modern. Because so little excavation has been undertaken it is impossible to compare Dark Age building traditions with those of medieval and later times to see whether there is any continuity. However, one might very tentatively suggest potential Dark Age origins for one of the most familiar types of traditional building in the modern Lakeland landscape, the bank barn (see pp169-70 and Plate 39). Bank barns, generally built into sloping ground, have threshing floors and barns at an upper level and byres and stables below, with an upper entrance to the barn on one side and separate access to the lower level on the other. In Britain bank barns are only frequent within the Lake District. The oldest surviving examples appear to date from the seventeenth century and so far there is no evidence for their earlier existence in the area but it is curious that this type of building is so characteristic of this particular area and that the closest parallels to it are in Norway!

4

THE FARMING LANDSCAPE

FARMSTEAD, FIELD AND FELL

IMAGINE in your mind's eye that you have scrambled part-way up a fellside to drink in the view down a Lakeland valley in the rain-washed air and low sunlight of an autumn afternoon. The texture of the landscape – the ribs of rock on the high fells; the swell of drift-covered landforms in the valley bottom – and the way that human activity is constrained by and related to the underlying terrain are strikingly apparent. After regaining your breath and marvelling at the majesty of light and shade on the fell tops, your eye drops to the inhabited valley below. Spread out along the narrow valley floor and lapping the lower fellsides is a landscape of upland farms: a scatter of white-washed steadings; a patchwork of small, green fields divided by hedges and drystone walls and interrupted by wooded, rocky knolls; and, surrounding all, the rough fellside pastures, in some places enclosed by walls, in others lying open to the rock-strewn fells. It is the product, directly or indirectly, of the way countless generations have eked out a living from the comparatively inhospitable environment of the Lake District. This chapter is concerned essentially with three aspects of the landscape: the development of the *settlement pattern*, the scatter of farms, hamlets and cottages; the evolution of *field patterns* and land use on the improvable farmland in the valleys; and the ways in which past generations have exploited and managed the various *resources of the fells* themselves.

Before turning to chart the influence of successive generations of farming communities over the past nine hundred years, it is perhaps worth giving some thought to the landscape we see today. It is a composite entity, almost any part of it containing elements dating from widely different periods. Even where the 'fabric' of the buildings, walls, woods and hedgerows we see today is comparatively young, the position of a building or the line of a field boundary was often determined by events in the much more distant past and may thus preserve the memory of much older patterns. As we shall see, the *sites* of many farmsteads, the *lines* of many field walls and tracks are almost certainly medieval in origin, even if repeated renovation means that most of what we see today dates from within the last two hundred years.

The farming landscape should thus be seen as a rolling, dynamic entity, a multi-period legacy from the past which continues to be modified. And yet the strict environmental controls on farming, imposed by terrain, poor soils and climate, have endowed the Lakeland landscape with something of a timeless quality, in that physical constraints have determined that the basic patterns of land use have remained broadly stable over the centuries. Improvable, 'farmed' land was, and to a large extent still is, restricted to the better-drained soils of the valley floors and lower slopes of the fells, while the fellsides, whether steep and thin-soiled or water-logged and acidic, offered little scope for improvement and remain in large part as rough grazing land. One of the most striking features of the view in rain-washed autumn sunshine is the sharp contrast in colour between the soft greens of the valley-bottom fields and the blazing red-brown of dead bracken on the fellside. The clear-cut vegetational boundary is largely the result of centuries of contrasting land management either side of the wall dividing farmland from fell – the 'head-dyke', to use the Scottish term – a line often marking the point where thinning soils and increasing slope dictated the limit of improvable land. Until the enclosure of some fell grazings by Act of Parliament in the nineteenth century, the head-dyke was perhaps the fundamental division in the farming landscape of the Lake District. It remains so in places like Langdale and Borrowdale, where the fells are still open common grazings. Although it often coincided with the limit of improvable land, the head-dyke was not the limit of human influence on the landscape. It was, rather, the boundary between the two complementary components of the Lakeland community's landed resources, the farmland of the valley floor yielding crops of corn and hay, and the open pastures of the fellsides. In tracing the development of the Lakeland farming landscape, we are thus looking at how the farming community managed its resources on both sides of the head-dyke.

THE MEDIEVAL FOUNDATIONS: 1150–1550

After the Norman Conquest (which was completed in Cumbria only after the conquest of the 'land of Carlisle' in 1092) the increasing volume of documentary evidence enables us to gain a firmer impres-

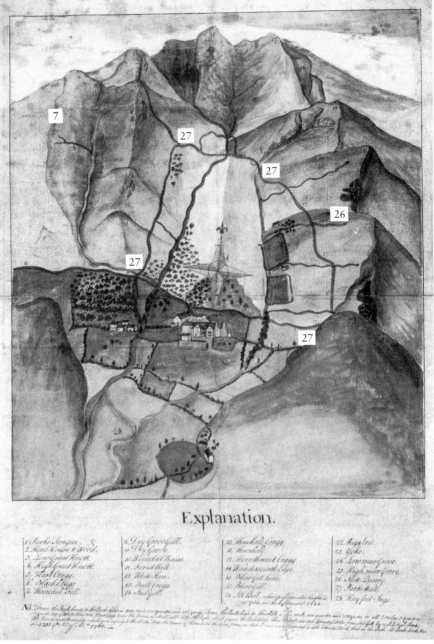

A SOUTH-PROSPECT OF TROUTBECK PARKE.

Explanation.

1. Parke Tongue
2. Herd House & Wood.
3. Low Great Knott.
4. High Great Knott.
5. Hart Crags.
6. Black Crags.
7. Woundal Fell

8. Dry Grove Gill.
9. Dry Grove.
10. Woundal Raise.
11. Scrival Nab.
12. White Howe.
13. Ball Crags.
14. Sadgill.

15. Threshele Cragg.
16. Threshele.
17. Thornthwait Cragg.
18. Wandesworth Edge.
19. Blew gill howe.
20. Blewgill.
21. St Bell where perpindicular hight is 200 yards on the slopewardst 244.

22. Rigg End.
23. Yoke.
24. Low mar Greve.
25. High mar Greve.
26. Slate Quarry.
27. Parke wall.
28. Hay foot Ings.

N.B. From the Parke howse to the Parke hed is one mile one quarter and 30 yards; from the Parke hed to Thresheld is one mile one quarter and 30 yards; in all 2 miles 3 quarters...

Plate 19 Troutbeck Park: a remarkable bird's-eye view of the farm in the mid eighteenth century. Troutbeck Park originated as a medieval deer park belonging to the barons of Kendal: the line marked '27' is the park wall encompassing the Tongue and the valleys of Trout Beck and Hagg Gill. Many elements of the field pattern

sion of the evolution of the rural landscape we see today. The key to understanding the development of the farming landscape as the valleys were settled and dales communities became established during the Middle Ages lies in the framework of feudal lordship in Cumbria. The pattern was one of great baronial estates, anchored on lordly seats in the lowlands (such as the castles of Greystoke, Kendal, Millom, Egremont and Cockermouth), but embracing within their boundaries large sections of the Lake District. The barony of Kendal, for instance, included all the valleys of southern Westmorland from Langdale to Longsleddale; the estate centred on Millom embraced all the fells between the Esk and the Duddon; that centred on Cockermouth all of 'Derwentfells', the mountainous country between the Derwent and Cocker valleys. The pattern of lordship was ostensibly established in the aftermath of the Norman Conquest, but some of the baronies may well have been reincarnations of pre-Conquest estates. By the time the written record becomes more plentiful in the thirteenth century the mountainous Lakeland areas of nearly all the great estates were described as private 'forest' or 'free chase', that is as hunting preserves belonging to the great baronial overlords. The medieval terminology is preserved on the modern map in such names as Skiddaw Forest, Copeland Forest, Fawcett Forest and Ralphland Forest. The term 'forest' did not imply that the fells were necessarily densely wooded in the early Middle Ages – though they contained considerably greater stretches of woodland then than in later centuries – it referred rather to the upland areas' distinctive legal status by which the overlords could exercise controls to preserve the game. In practice, however, the earliest detailed estate records of the private forests of the Lake District in the later thirteenth century suggest that the lords were interested less in conservation for hunting than in the exploitation of the upland pastures for stock farming. By encouraging or, at least, tolerating peasant colonists, and by exploiting the fell pastures directly by establishing large demesne stock farms (farms managed directly for the lords themselves), the lords ensured that the frontier of settlement was pushed deep into the Lake District during the Middle Ages and the framework of much of the modern settlement pattern was laid.

Plate 19 cont
survive today, but significant landscape change has also taken place since c1750: the open fells round Woundale (labelled '7') were divided and enclosed in 1842; Hird House, the cluster of buildings to the left of the main farmstead, is now a solitary barn; the buildings at the foot of the painting have disappeared entirely; the woodland on the flanks of the Tongue has been considerably reduced in extent; and the single small slate quarry (labelled '26') has been swallowed up by the much larger workings of the nineteenth century *(Reproduced by permission of the National Trust).*

Although whole valleys were in theory embraced by the private forests, there was often a division by the later thirteenth century between the lower reaches, where peasant colonisation was taking place, and the daleheads, over which the feudal overlords retained direct control. The daleheads, where hay meadows on the valley floor were ringed by fellside pastures, were exploited in a variety of ways. Some lords established dairy farms, known as 'vaccaries', which were managed by their own officials. In the western valleys there were vaccaries at Wasdale Head, at the head of Ennerdale, and at Gatesgarth, at the head of Buttermere, by the early fourteenth century. The last is the best-documented in the Lake District: in the 1280s it supported a herd of forty milch cows and their offspring, and was thus similar in size to the vaccaries established in the forests of Pendle and Rossendale in the Lancashire Pennines. Other lords derived income from 'agistment', the grazing of other people's stock on their dalehead pastures. Private pastures such as these were recorded at Grisedale and Martindalehead, at the head of Ullswater, in 1362, and stock were being agisted in Troutbeck Park, at the head of the Troutbeck valley, by 1283. In other places dalehead land was donated to religious houses. On such grants the abbeys of Fountains and Furness founded vaccaries at Stonethwaite in Borrowdale and Brotherilkeld at the head of Eskdale, respectively. By these means the dalehead pastures and meadows were retained in the hands of great landholders, whether lay or monastic, and the uppermost reaches of many valleys were preserved from colonisation by peasant farmers in the thirteenth century. The landscape of these lordly farms has, of course, undergone great modification in later centuries as they were leased out and often divided between tenant farmers in the later Middle Ages. But some memories of their distinctive origins remain. It is striking, for example, how there exist in many of the daleheads large, convex enclosures embracing whole banks of fellside. The Deer Forest at the head of Martindale; Gatesgarth Side on the slopes of Robinson above Buttermere; The Side and Siver Cove at the head of Ennerdale: all are probably associated with the demesne status of these daleheads, where herds of cattle grazed alongside surviving herds of deer in the thirteenth century. Another memory survives in the ear-marks of sheep flocks on some dalehead farms. At Gatesgarth, Brotherilkeld, Gillerthwaite in Ennerdale, and Troutbeck Park, for example, the phrase 'cropped both ears' in the *Shepherd's Guides* betrays their origin as lordly farms, the cropping of both ears (the most extreme and unalterable ear-mark) being reserved for the lord of the manor's flock.

Outside the upper reaches of the valleys, peasant colonisation was the principal agent in establishing the framework of the settlement pattern. The twelfth and thirteenth centuries were a period of sustained population growth and almost every English county contains farms and hamlets whose lands were carved from the wild at that time. In the Lake District a major aspect of this tide of colonisation appears to have involved the conversion of shielings or *saetrs*, temporary dwellings on land used as summer pasture, into permanent farms (see also Chapter 3). Glimpses of the process can be gleaned in documents concerning two remote valleys in the forest of Derwentfells in the late thirteenth century. The first is Wythop, tucked into the fells to the west of Bassenthwaite Lake, which had been used solely for grazing c1260 but had grown into a settled community by 1307. The lord of Wythop had to buy out pasture rights belonging to neighbouring landowners to allow enclosure to take place, and the modern map provides evidence of the valley's former use as a shieling ground in the names Old Scales ('the old shielings') and Lord's Seat ('the lord's *saetr* or summer pasture ground'). The second area is the significantly-named Newlands valley, south of Braithwaite. Estate accounts record the taking-in of new fields from the fellsides in the years between 1266 and 1310. Again, there are several place-names which record the valley's former use as a shieling ground: the older name for the Newlands valleys was Rogersett ('Roger's *saetr*'), and the element *scale* ('a shieling hut') is contained in the farm names Gutherscale, Skelgill, and Keskadale. As we have seen, both *saetr* and *scale* were terms brought to the Lake District by the Scandinavian settlers.

These two valleys are probably unusual only in that the process of colonisation is recorded in surviving documentary sources. Most of the numerous farms and hamlets whose names include the element 'scale' probably represent similar conversions of shielings to permanent farms in the twelfth or thirteenth centuries, and it is very likely that many of the 'thwaite' names also date from the major expansion of settlement at that time, rather than the initial period of Scandinavian colonisation (see Chapter 3). As in other parts of the country, much of the new settlement took the form of small hamlets and scattered farms, filling in the spaces between established communities. In the Cocker valley farms had been established in the villages of Buttermere and Lorton by the end of the twelfth century (and probably long before) and the wave of colonisation added new farms along the lower fellsides behind them: the hamlets of Armaside, Gillbrea, High Side, Scales and Swinside at Lorton and the arc of farms behind Buttermere village (Wood House, Crag Houses and Bowderbeck) all originated as new settlements in the century or so before 1300 (see Fig 12).

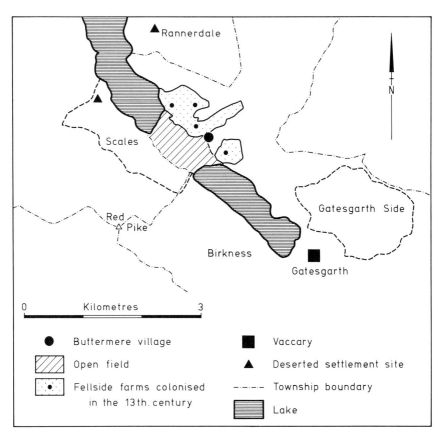

Fig 12 Buttermere: the medieval landscape.
Buttermere had many features typical of medieval Lakeland. The village, anchored on an open field on the alluvial flats between the lakes, was probably an early nucleus of settlement; the scattered farms around it were the product of colonisation in the thirteenth century. At Gatesgarth, at the head of the valley, was a large dairy farm (or 'vaccary'), belonging to the feudal overlord, and it is likely that the banks of fellside called Gatesgarth Side and Birkness were also demesne pastures. Scales, an area containing late-surviving woodland on the slopes of Red Pike, was probably a shieling ground and contains an extensive deserted medieval settlement, possibly an industrial hamlet

By 1300 the Lake District valleys were well peopled. The oak woods which had supported the herds of pigs recorded in such names as Swinside, Swindale and Grisdale were dwindling, partly through deliberate clearance, but largely through failure of regeneration as a result of trampling by the settlers' flocks and herds. The shieling grounds where cattle had formerly grazed in the summer now supported permanent farms and the valley communities were swelled by the presence of numerous cottagers making a living by various means, such as wood-turning, charcoal-burning, iron smelting, tanning, mining, fishing and weaving.

Soon after 1300 the era of colonisation was brought abruptly to a halt by a century and more of what has been termed 'war and pestilence'; war in the form of the devastation wrought by successive Scottish raids as the comparative harmony of the Border in the thirteenth century was shattered; and pestilence in the Black Death of 1348–9 and later outbreaks of plague. Certainly, the tide of destruction wrought by Scottish armed bands washed repeatedly round the northern and eastern edges of the Lake District and, in 1315 and 1322, flowed down the western margins and into Furness but, in general, the communities of the Lake District proper escaped direct attack. Much more serious to the stock-rearing farmers of medieval Lakeland must have been the series of devastating cattle plagues and sheep 'murrain', together with the probability of frequent harvest failure, not only in the famine years of 1315–17 but also more generally as the climate became cooler and wetter during the fourteenth century. Documents which throw light on Lakeland communities in the 1320s, 1330s and 1340s portray a landscape containing impoverished and 'debilitated' inhabitants, untenanted houses, and fields reverting to the wild. Although we know hardly anything about its effects in the Lake District, the Black Death, when it came, struck at dalesfolk already depleted and weakened by several decades of hardship.

The scale of settlement desertion in the period 1300 to 1450 is difficult to assess, partly because, in an environment where cultivable land was so severely restricted, much of the abandoned land, and some farmstead sites, would have been reclaimed and reused in the Tudor period. There are, however, some earthworks which may indicate the presence of marginal land which went out of use in the fourteenth century and has never been ploughed since. Although we cannot be certain of their date, the flights of terraced lynchets on steep hillsides at Sleddale Grange in Wet Sleddale and behind Old Scales in Wythop may perhaps date from this period. Some deserted settlement sites are known as well. Two of the most extensive, at Scale Beck, Buttermere, and Smithy Beck, Ennerdale, may have been iron-working hamlets, rather than agricultural settlements. They would tend to confirm the evidence of rentals which suggest that the cottagers, who had formed a significant part of many Lakeland communities in the thirteenth century, had declined almost to extinction by the sixteenth.

The depression continued until c1450 when a revival in the economy of the Lake District generated another phase of land-taking which lasted until the later sixteenth century. The growth of the woollen cloth industry in the Kendal area and in High Furness both stimulated a demand for wool and provided a means of livelihood to supplement farming. Population levels appear to have risen sharply and to have stimulated a thirst for land which could be quenched only by taking in new land from the waste or by splitting existing holdings. It appears that the thirteenth-century expansion of settlement had almost reached the limits of improvable land in the restricted environment of the Lake District, so that most new enclosures in the century 1450 to 1550 were small 'intakes', nibbling at the fellsides along the head-dyke or creating small islands of farmland on patches of better land at a distance from the body of enclosure in the valley. In some places members of the farming community joined forces to separate larger blocks of land from the fell, often as enclosed pasture rather than ploughland. At Braithwaite, near Keswick, for example, nine tenants enclosed Braithwaite How, the hill behind the village, as a shared pasture c1480; the villagers of Low Lorton enclosed an area of moorland called 'Lorton Head' in the valley bottom between Lorton and Brackenthwaite in the 1470s; while on Bleak Rigg, deep in the fells behind Buttermere, the tumbled remains of a stone-faced bank are all that remain of the efforts of nine local farmers who enclosed it c1568. The limits of practicable enclosure, whether dictated by the physical environment or by the need to keep open sufficient common grazing land for the community as a whole, were reached by this period of intaking in much of the Lake District. When this occurred the growing population of the southern parts of the district could only be kept on the land by dividing holdings between members of a family. By 1550 half holdings, so generated, are common in rentals, especially in Furness, southern Westmorland and south-west Cumberland. It should be noted that the farms bearing 'Ground' names in High Furness and the Lickle valley, which have been interpreted in the past as originating in the early sixteenth century, are more likely to have been established initially in the great wave of colonisation in the thirteenth century, even if their names (Walker Ground, Stephenson Ground, for example) record those of their Tudor owners.

Another change in the late-medieval period which has left its mark in the modern landscape was the attempt to preserve the acreage of surviving woodland and the development of active ways of managing woodland resources. The stimulus was the increasing demand for charcoal for the iron industry and for the smelting of lead and copper ores. From the fifteenth century we find evidence for the fencing of woodland against stock and its management on a coppice rotation. The steady attrition to which woodland had been subjected for centuries was thereby reduced and enclosed coppice woods, often on rocky outcrops, became a feature of the landscape of many Lakeland valleys.

THE LANDSCAPE OF THE 'STATESMEN: 1550–1750

In the sixteenth century the nature of the documentary evidence available to the landscape historian changes and it becomes possible to reconstruct the farming landscape in some detail at the local level and to recapture something of the way it functioned. In the literature on the history of the Lake District the period 1550 to 1750 has become known as the age of 'statesmen', (from 'estatesmen'), the small family farmers whose customary tenure gave them a security tantamount to that on freehold land, generating the sturdy independence of spirit noted by the Lake Poets and other late eighteenth-century writers. The division of the valley bottoms into numerous small estates was an important factor in determining the history of the human landscape of the Lake District, since the power to change the landscape lay firmly in the hands of the 'statesmen farmers and the lord of the manor's influence was severely limited by the strength of the tenants' customary rights. By 1500 the vaccaries and almost all other lands formerly retained in hand by the great lords had been let to tenants so that 'statesman influence was almost ubiquitous and the farming landscape developed slowly and in piecemeal fashion across the Tudor and Stuart periods.

Estate surveys, such as that prepared for the Earl of Northumberland in 1578, give some idea of the variety of farming landscapes in the valley bottoms by the later sixteenth century. The way in which a community's farmland was apportioned between individual farmers was partly a product of the constraints imposed by the physical environment and partly the result of the way the settlement pattern had evolved in the medieval period. The broad rule was that, where there was a sufficiently extensive area of potential ploughland or good hay meadow on the valley floor, communal organisation of farmland was to be found. Small 'townfields', areas of open arable land and meadow in which several farmers held unfenced strips, were to be found on many of the wider delta flats, usually associated with a clustered grouping of farmsteads into a hamlet or small village. Such open fields are recorded at Coniston, Grasmere, Braithwaite, Buttermere and Lorton, for example. At Braithwaite, the Earl's survey of 1578 describes a community of sixteen farms set in an open landscape in which most land was held as unfenced shares. An open arable field, divided into several furlongs, covered the apron of drier land immediately east of the village. Beyond it, where poor soil drainage defeated the plough on the wet valley floor beside Newlands Beck, were a number of shared hay meadows, while to the north lay Braithwaite Moss, a peat-filled hollow in which each farm held a share of peat-moss for fuel. Finally, there were three enclosures of rough pasture, the largest being Braithwaite How, the hillock behind the village, in which groups of farmers held shares. In short, almost every category of land at Braithwaite was held in open shares, even if there was little regularity in the way those shares were distributed between holdings.

The land-holding pattern at Braithwaite and other valley-floor villages represents one end of a spectrum. At the opposite end was the isolated farmstead set in a ring-fenced block of enclosed fields, though such farms were comparatively rare. In most valleys a group of between three and eight farms was the typical unit of land organisation, whether the farmsteads were clustered into a hamlet or dispersed across the valley. Even where most land was held as separate enclosures rather than unfenced strips, a farmer's fields often lay scattered among the closes of his neighbours, so that each had land of variable quality. As an example, we may take the four sixteenth-century farms at Powter How, a couple of miles north of Braithwaite (Fig 13). In 1578 they were all held, at identical rents, by members of the Wood family, suggesting that they may have originated in the splitting of a single holding. All four held shares in a close of ploughland called Low Rood and had pieces of peat moss in Braithwaite Moss. Three of the farms also shared the rocky hillock, Powter How Wood, under which the farmsteads lay, and, with Wood End farm, shared a pasture close called Windyhill, on the lower slopes of Barf. Otherwise, their holdings consisted of small fields scattered along the narrow strip of land between the mountains and the lake. Woodland and rough pasture excluded, each farm contained little more than ten acres of land.

The evidence of probate inventories shows us that the Wood family were typical of 'statesman society. On their small acreage of valley-bottom land they cultivated crops of oats and bigg (a barley) and mowed the vital crop of hay to sustain their livestock through the winter. That livestock, the mainstay of their economy, consisted typically of a herd of between 10 and 20 cattle, a horse or two, and a flock of sheep. Some small farmers had fewer than 50 sheep, but the 140 sheep owned by Thomas Wood of Powter How when he died in 1579 was not uncommon. The products of a pastoral economy also enabled members of Lakeland communities to supplement their income by engaging in crafts or domestic industries. Spinning and weaving took place on many farms, particularly in the southern valleys, while the Woods, like others in the Keswick area, harvested oak bark from their wooded pastures and were tanners.

The pastures of the open fells beyond the head-dyke were an integral part of the 'statesman's farm. They provided grazing for his sheep all

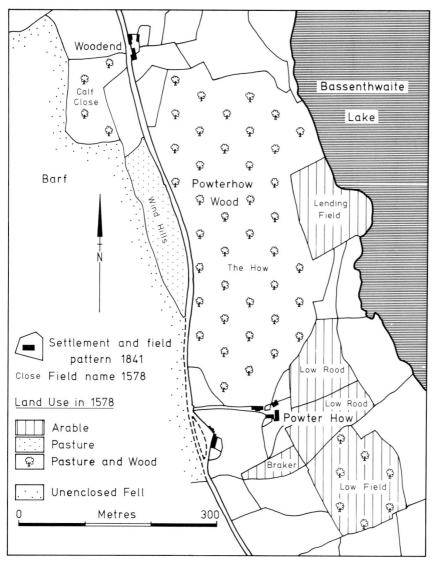

Fig 13 Powter How, Thornthwaite: the farming landscape of a Tudor hamlet

the year round and for his cattle and horses in summer, and also
yielded other resources, notably peat (for fuel) and bracken (for
thatching, cattle bedding, and burning into potash). By the sixteenth
century the open fells had largely come to be treated as 'manorial
waste', their distinctive status as private forest having been forgotten.
Manorial waste was unenclosed and unimproved land, legally vested
in the lord of the manor but encumbered by the common rights of the
tenants in the manor. The principal common rights exercised by the
'statesman communities were those of pasture, the right to graze on

87

the fells those animals a farmer could overwinter on the produce of his farmland; and turbary, the right to dig peat for fuel and sods for the repair of hedge banks and house roofs. In theory the rights were general to the whole waste and no one farmer had exclusive rights to one particular part of it. In practice, however, the manor courts, which oversaw the day-to-day management of the fell land, upheld customs and laid down byelaws which divided the fells into much smaller units reflecting both farming needs and the suitability of different types of fell land for different purposes.

The complexity of land-use patterns on the fells is illustrated by the decisions recorded in 1587 and 1664 by courts in the manor of Eskdale, Miterdale and Wasdale Head. The extensive acreage of waste in the manor fell into three distinct categories: the steep banks of the lower fellsides which hem in the tongues of improvable dale-bottom land in each valley; the wet moorland plateau between Miterdale and Eskdale and in the saddle surrounding Burnmoor Tarn; and the rugged high fells encompassing such peaks as Yewbarrow, Kirk Fell, and Sca Fell itself. The manor court orders spelt out how the varied resources of this vast mountain acreage were to be exploited and illustrate how communal custom reinforced the threefold natural division into 'the Banks', 'the Moor', and 'the Fells'. The Banks, the steep but low altitude grazing land close to the farms (now largely smothered with bracken), were the most prized fell land and were strictly preserved as cow pastures on which milking cows were kept during the summer. In Eskdale and Miterdale each farm had its own cow pasture on the steep bank behind it. This area came to be regarded as the exclusive right of the farm to the extent that many cow pastures in these valleys had been enclosed by their 'owners' by the end of the seventeenth century. They are represented in the modern landscape by the large stone-walled intakes such as those on the fellsides behind Spout House and Wha House in Eskdale. At Wasdale Head management of the Banks was even more strictly regulated. The inhabitants complained in 1659 of a desperate shortage of good pasture and claimed that they were 'forced to put their milch kine and all other their Cattell to the Common to their great dammage they not being able there to subsist without serving them with nettles and other weeds'. In 1664 the manor court ordered that only cows actually in milk and one horse per farm were to be grazed on the Banks.

The second category of fell land, the Moor or Burn Moor, in the saddle between Eskdale and Wasdale Head, was reserved for the whole manorial community as a pasture for horses, bullocks, heifers, and dry cows. It was not enclosed by a physical boundary but its limits

Plate 20 Wasdale Head from Westmorland Cairn on Great Gable. An isolated patch of cultivable land hemmed in by steep mountainsides. The farms here enter the written record in the fourteenth century when the dalehead contained four 'vaccaries', large dairy farms belonging to the baron of Egremont. By the sixteenth century Wasdale Head contained eighteen farms, each consisting of a small patch of ploughland and meadow in an open field covering the valley floor, and common rights on the vast fellside pastures. The patchwork of walled fields, most of which were in existence by 1795, is the result of piecemeal enclosure of the open field, while the larger rectangular enclosures on the lower skirts of the fells are 'intakes', probably dating from the eighteenth century *(W. Rollinson)*

were specified in detail by the manor court in 1587. Finally, there were the high fells on which the sheep flocks scraped a living in the summer months. In Eskdale and Miterdale individual holdings or small groups of farms each had a separate heaf, a known and delimited bank of fell on which its sheep grazed. On the western flanks of Sca Fell, for example, were three heafs: Hard Rigg, the grazing ground of the flocks of Spout House and Borrowdale Place; Broad Tongue, the heaf for Hows, Gill Bank and Paddockwray farms; and Quagrigg, reserved for the sheep of the tenants of Boot. The high fells around Wasdale Head were also divided into heafs, though it is not clear whether the sheep of a particular farm were restricted to a particular heaf. The seven blocks of fellside encircling the dalehead were each treated as a separate heaf in 1664: Green How; Lingmell; 'Coves' (the arc of mountainside between Great Gable and Scafell Pikes); Kirk Fell; 'betwixt becks' (the flanks of Pillar between Mosedale and Gatherstone becks); 'Caplecragg' (the flanks of Red Pike); and Yewbarrow. The complexity of arrangements such as these clearly required farmers to move their stock long distances and made necessary the acceptance of customary drift ways or 'out rakes', routes from each farm out to its heaf on the fells. Some of these ancient routes are preserved on the modern map in the network of public rights of way reaching from the valleys deep into the fells.

Pasture was not the only common right which had to be regulated by the manor courts. With the destruction of woodland during the medieval period, common of turbary, the right to cut peat for fuel, became increasingly important. Deposits of peat were not distributed evenly across the fells and the usual arrangement was for each farm to have its own 'peat pot' where fuel could be cut in May. In valleys such as Eskdale and Mardale the peat diggings lay on a wet plateau several hundred feet above the valley floor and 'peat scales' or 'peat cotes', small drystone huts in which peats were stored and dried, were built by individual farmers out on the fells. On the low fells around Eskdale the remains of over thirty such huts survive, often built beside a holding's drift way onto the fell. Bracken, the curse of the modern Lakeland farmer, was also harvested from the fells by the 'statesmen. The right to cut it seems never to have been challenged and, indeed, the demand for it, for thatching, stock bedding, and burning into ash for soap-making, led again to tight control through the manor courts. In many manors individual farms had exclusive rights over defined banks of bracken, their shares in this valuable resource being known as 'bracken dalts' or 'bracken rooms'.

Apart from the construction and repair of tracks, sheep folds and peat huts, the human impact on the landscape of the fells was largely an indirect influence, the cumulative result of the exercise of common rights over the centuries. In ecological terms we may think of a slow but steady removal of nutrients from the soils of the fells as countless generations of sheep and cattle grazed and, in places, overgrazed the vegetation. But there were also more direct human influences: in Der-wentfells, for example, the burning of heather to improve the pasture is recorded from the early sixteenth century, when the inhabitants of Thornthwaite and Lorton were charged with unlawful 'haythburns'. The exercise of turbary rights could have a detrimental effect on the quality of land. Although strict rules attempted to limit the flooding of worked peat deposits and the stripping of turf from land particularly sensitive to erosion (as that immediately outside the head-dyke, for example), it is likely that peat- and turf-cutting caused a steady de-terioration in land quality.

The era of the 'statesman has so far been portrayed as a static picture of unchanging traditional farming. Yet the period 1550 to 1750 saw some major changes which left their mark on the Lakeland landscape. The population growth of the sixteenth century appears to have slowed down by 1600 and many Lake District communities declined in size during the seventeenth and early eighteenth centuries. The resulting easing of the pressure on land heralded the beginning of a process which has continued almost to the present day, namely the gradual reduction in the number of farms as holdings have been thrown together into larger units. The process accelerated during the nineteenth and twentieth centuries and most valleys contain the tumbled ruins of farmsteads deserted since 1850. There was, however, a slow but steady process of farm desertion across the 'statesman period as well. Two extreme examples of the accumulation of land in fewer hands come from the western valleys: at Wasdale Head the eighteen holdings of 1578 dropped to fourteen by 1650, ten by 1750 and only eight by 1800. In the early nineteenth century William Green commented that 'the vestiges of many ruined cottages show that this village was once more considerable'. In the neighbouring valley of Miterdale a community of six farms in 1578 had been reduced to three by 1750 and the footings of two farmsteads near Bakerstead and Miterdale Head (steadings themselves abandoned during the nineteenth century) are tangible reminders of the decline of this small, remote community in the century after 1650. These valleys, poor and remote from the areas of contemporary economic growth – textiles in the Kendal area; iron-making in Furness; coal and tobacco trading in West Cumberland – are admittedly extreme cases but they serve as a reminder that change was an ever-present feature of 'statesman society. Even Wordsworth, who helped to create the romantic illusion of a stable 'Golden Age' in Lake District society before 1750, noted that the 'union of several tenements' in the hands of one proprietor was a common feature in the seventeenth century.

Changes also occurred in the landscape of field boundaries in the valley bottoms. The open fields and shared closes recorded in the sixteenth century were gradually enclosed, the shares of different farmers being separated by physical boundaries. Much of this enclosure took place in piecemeal fashion as small groups of farmers agreed to consolidate strips in an open field and to fence their shares, or to divide an open hay meadow or enclosed pasture between themselves. In consequence, many of these landscape changes were never recorded in writing. Where more than a few farmers were involved, as in the larger open fields of villages around the edges of the Lake District, more formal measures were needed and there survive manor court orders decreeing that enclosure should take place. At Yanwath, near Penrith,

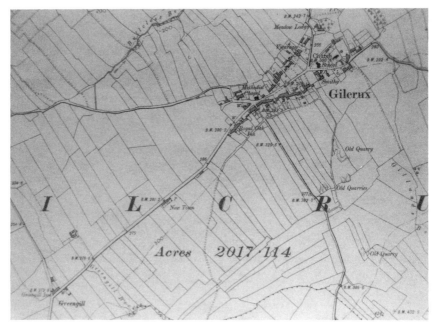

Plate 21 Gilcrux, on the Cumberland lowlands inland from Maryport, as shown on the 1900 edition of the Ordnance Survey 6″ map. The very narrow, strip-like fields on either side of the village are the 'infields', enclosed by order of the manor court in 1648. The more rectangular fields between the roads running out from the west end of the village are the result of later enclosure of the 'outfield' and common grazings, the final phase of which was the enclosure of Gilcrux Common in 1814

for example, the manor court ordered in 1567 'thatt every tenaunte shall Exchaynge theyre landes yn the feldes One with Anotherr So that every tenaunte may have theyre tenementes yn Severall Closes', but the order seems to have been only partly successful as, even in 1584, parts of the fields there remained open. At Gilcrux, in the Ellen valley inland from Maryport, it was agreed in 1648

> to make devision of the Infeild grounds now in Neighbourhood, by measure and lotts proportionably according to the vallew of every man's ground, to be laid together, every man's by itselfe, and to have each of them their proportion of hedge accordingly laid sever-ally by themselves.

The result at Gilcrux was the creation of a pattern of curving, strip-like fields to the north and south of the village, a new landscape of enclo-sure which preserved in its field boundaries the lines of strips and furlongs in the former open fields (see Plate 21). A glance at the modern 1:25,000 map shows that similar, strip field patterns, almost certainly the legacy of enclosure during this period, are found in many parts of the Eden Valley and Cumberland plain.

In the Lake District proper there are fewer glimpses of the process of enclosure in the documentary record, though scattered examples may be cited. At Low Lorton, for example, part of the open field which lay unenclosed in 1578 had been fenced up by 1649; at Mockerkin, near Loweswater, the manor court heard in 1685 how enclosure of a block of land called 'Bramaryes' had disturbed an accustomed right of way; at Satterthwaite in High Furness a series of agreements in the years around 1720, preserved in the title deeds of the Chamney family, record the exchange of shares in open arable land as the constituent parts of a holding were consolidated and, we may assume, enclosed.

THE AGE OF IMPROVEMENT: 1750–1870

During the latter part of the eighteenth century and the first half of the nineteenth the spirit of agricultural improvement which swept through Britain's landowning classes resulted in the re-writing of the landscape of large parts of the country. As has already been noted, the physical limitations to large-scale 'scientific' agriculture and the fragmentation of landownership into numerous small yeoman estates protected much of the Lake District from wholesale change and, in general, the farmland of the valley floors remains 'ancient landscape' which has evolved piecemeal across the centuries. Side by side with its 'ancient' farmland, however, the Lake District also contains large areas of 'planned landscape', where the human features were determined by the careful deliberations of draughtsman and surveyor in the century after 1750. For the most part the planned landscape is restricted to the fell land outside the head-dyke, large parts of which were enclosed by Act of Parliament in the nineteenth century, though there are some areas where an improving landlord, spurred either by the spirit of improvement or by the new fashion for mountain scenery, transformed the older farmland of a corner of Lakeland in the period 1750 to 1870.

Parliamentary Enclosure was both a fundamental land reform, disentangling the balance of rights between lord and tenants on manorial waste and replacing it by a pattern of enclosed fields in individual ownership, and, potentially at least, a change in land use. Once the common grazings had been enclosed, they could be improved, drained, and cultivated if position and inherent fertility allowed. Enclosure of Lakeland wastes was spread over a long period, the more improvable commons around the edge of the fells being enclosed from the later eighteenth century, the barren fellsides of the heart of the Lake District either being enclosed in the final phases of the movement in the middle decades of the nineteenth century, or remaining unenclosed to this day. The first burst of Parliamentary Enclosure in Cumbria occurred in the 1760s and 1770s, when a spate of enclosure awards carved up lowland moors along the edges of the Lake District from West Cumberland round to the Eden Valley: Harrington moor was enclosed in 1761; Distington in 1768; Bassenthwaite in 1771; Sebergham in 1765; Castle Sowerby in 1769; Kings Meaburn in 1777; Ormside in 1772. In each case reclamation for arable cultivation was the prime objective, as it was in the second phase of enclosure during the Napoleonic Wars, when inflated grain prices encouraged farmers to increase the acreage under the plough. In Cumberland and Westmorland alone no fewer than forty-seven awards were executed in the decade starting in 1810, and a further thirty-three were made in the 1820s. Most divided moorland peripheral to the Lake District proper, though the tide of enclosure in those years washed well round the margins of the fells and, in places, penetrated the heartland, as in the enclosure of Thornthwaite and Underskiddaw commons, near Keswick, in 1814 and 1815 respectively. The enthusiasm for land improvement in those years led John Christian Curwen of Workington, one of the pioneering improvers in Cumbria, to comment, in his presidential report to the Workington Agricultural Society for 1812, on the 'disposition to carry the plough much nearer heaven than what was ever dreamed of a few years ago'.

An example of landscape created by the drive towards reclamation comes from Whinfell, on the north-western edge of the Lake District near Cockermouth, where the wastes – rough hill land rather than barren fellside – were enclosed in 1826 (Fig 14). The Commissioners sold pieces of the former common to defray the cost of producing the award. By purchasing two of these and two smaller allotments, John Nicholson, a gentleman farmer of The Hill, in Blindbothel, obtained a compact 184-acre block of hill land, rising to 1248ft (385m) on which he established a new farmstead called Hatteringill. The stone-walled enclosures still bear witness to the vast labours expended in paring, burning, harrowing and sowing the ground to make cultivable land that was formerly gorse-ridden rough pasture. Most of Nicholson's estate is covered with the straight, narrow ridge and furrow which survives so widely in northern England where marginal land was brought under the plough in the early nineteenth century. Circular stone platforms, known as 'stack bottoms', were built in the corners of the new fields to keep stooks of oats dry at harvest. Stones were cleared into rows and carted into heaps. In 1841 Hatteringill was occupied by the Nicholsons' tenants, a farming household of eight souls, but by

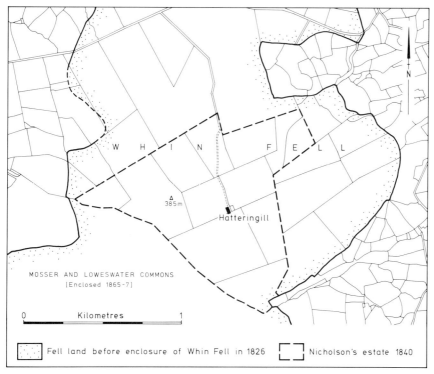

Fig 14 The landscape of Parliamentary Enclosure: Whinfell, Cumberland, enclosed in 1826

1851 the farm was uninhabited. On that wind-swept hill top Parliamentary Enclosure generated a short burst of agricultural activity, spanning little more than twenty years at most, and has left a legacy of abandoned features in the landscape today.

A third phase of enclosure occurred in the middle decades of the nineteenth century. Most of the enclosures of fell land in the heart of the Lake District date from these years: Watermillock, beside Ullswater, in 1835; Matterdale in 1882; Hartsop in 1865; Sleddale Forest, in 1849; Kentmere, in 1850; Applethwaite, Hugill and Troutbeck in 1842; Ennerdale in 1872; Loweswater in 1865. The landscape created by Parliamentary Enclosure was the epitome of deliberate planning: wide, straight public and occupation roads and rectilinear enclosures cutting across the land surface, apparently oblivious to the steepness of slope or the presence of crags. In most of the high fells the new enclosures were bounded by drystone walls, quarried locally by the itinerant wallers who built them. Many visitors to the Lake District still wonder at the herculean labour involved in their construction straight up a fellside or along the crest of the mountains. In the latest enclosures such as those of Ennerdale and Loweswater fells, within easy reach of the iron-making towns of West Cumberland, some farmers forsook

Plate 22 Landscape by design: Parliamentary Enclosure on Lorton Fell. The large, rectangular fields superimposed on the fells either side of Whinlatter Pass were laid out when the commons in Lorton township were enclosed in 1835. Improvement of the new fields on the lower slopes, and the establishment of the new farmstead of Darling How, visible in the middle distance, took place in the decades immediately after enclosure. The sharp outlines of the twentieth-century Forestry Commission plantations are dictated by the boundaries drawn by the enclosure commissioners in the 1830s *(A. J. L. Winchester)*

the stone wall for the new technology of iron fences. Less durable than walls, their gaunt remains, in the form of iron straining posts set in stones, still litter the slopes of Melbreak and the crests of High Crag, Haystacks and Brandreth. Little land improvement could be attempted on many of the high fells and the enclosures simply carved the former manorial waste into new property units. In one respect the full effect of Parliamentary Enclosure on the Lake District landscape was delayed for several generations. The fact that enclosure had taken place, allowing blocks of fell pasture to be bought and sold, was the necessary prerequisite for one significant land-use change, the afforestation of unimprovable fellsides. A few landowners planted their new allotments soon after enclosure – indeed, as early as 1861 the enclosure Commissioners claimed that Loweswater Fell would be 'much improved' by planting – but most afforestation took place under the auspices of the Forestry Commission in the middle decades of the twentieth century (see chapter 8). The straight-edged plantations of such forests as Whinlatter, Ennerdale and Blengdale, so disliked by the Friends of the Lake District, were determined by the allotment boundaries laid out by enclosure commissioners about a century before (see Plate 22).

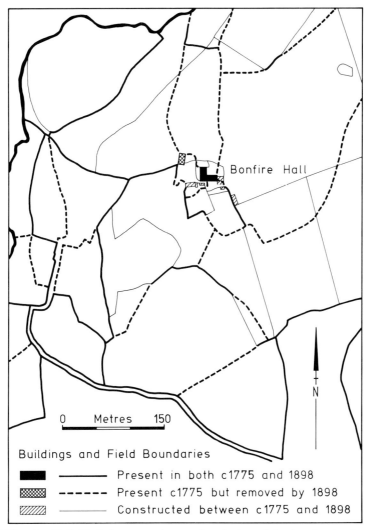

Fig 15 Bonfire Hall, Underbarrow: piecemeal evolution of the farming landscape in the nineteenth century

Parliamentary Enclosure thus created a completely new landscape on areas of former moorland and fell but left untouched the fields and woods of the valley bottoms. Many parts of this older landscape escaped a radical transformation in the later eighteenth or nineteenth century but that is not to say that they remained unchanged as successive generations of farmers tended their land. Many farm buildings date from the century after 1750; walls and hedges were repaired and renewed and, in places, fields were thrown together, or divided, or awkward corners removed, thus generating a steady stream of subtle changes to the landscape in detail. The cumulative effect of such piecemeal adjustments can be seen by comparing eighteenth-century

Plate 23 Higham Hall, an early nineteenth-century villa with a view across Bassenthwaite Lake to Skiddaw. The present house was built in 1827 for Thomas Hoskins on the site of an earlier farmhouse, which had been known simply as 'the High' or the 'Height', as it was the highest house on the hillside. Transformed into a neo-Gothic villa, the property was presumably thought to require a more impressive name *(A. J. L. Winchester)*

estate plans with the Ordnance Survey maps of the next century. The farm at Bonfire Hall, Underbarrow, near Kendal, may be taken as an example (Fig 15). Between the compilation of a plan of the estate c1775 and the 1898 edition of the Ordinance Survey plan, a surprisingly large number of small changes modified an area of countryside which, on the face of it, is a classic 'ancient' landscape. We should remember that the farming landscape of today has not been inherited unchanged from the days of the 'statesmen and that the field patterns of the valley bottoms have been subjected to a continual process of adjustment and renewal since 1750.

In some areas a more thorough re-writing took place as a result of what may be termed 'gentrification', where a member of the gentry or aristocracy converted part of the traditional farming landscape into that of a country villa set in parks and pleasure grounds. The result was to create a carefully contrived landscape of luxury, dictated by fashion (Plate 23). The fringes of the Lake District contain numerous examples of landscaped parkland attached to country seats. Some, such as those at Lowther, Levens and Holker, were the work of established local landowning families. Others, often on a much smaller scale, were created by rising local families who made their money in trade or industry. In the Lake District proper the product of gentrification was typically the lakeside villa, built by 'strangers in pursuit of beauty', as the Romantic movement led to the discovery of a taste for Lake District scenery during the late eighteenth century.

The first such villa was the Round House on Belle Isle, Windermere, built in 1774. Within twenty years numerous estates in picturesque lakeside situations had been bought by wealthy outsiders, their houses

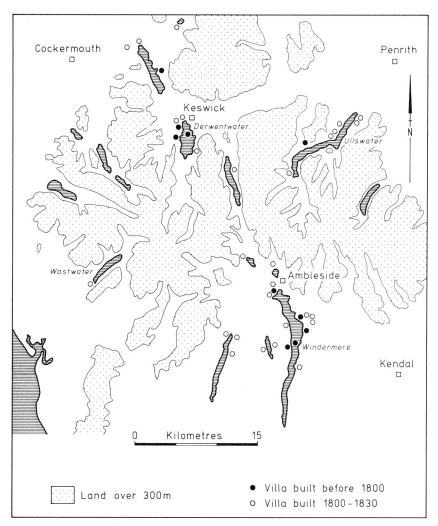

Fig 16 The quest for mountain scenery: villas in the Lake District before 1830

rebuilt, and the surrounding landscape of fields and woods carefully converted into gardens and parkland. The shores of Windermere and Derwentwater were the first to be transformed but even remote valleys like Wasdale had been discovered by the middle of the nineteenth century (Fig 16). The first generation of lakeside villas in the 1780s and 1790s included Calgarth, on Windermere, built for Richard Watson, Bishop of Llandaff; Lyulph's Tower, on Ullswater, a Gothic retreat built for the Duke of Norfolk; and the houses on Derwent Isle and at Derwent Bank and Barrow Cascade, on the shores of Derwentwater, built by Joseph Pocklington, the flamboyant member of a Newark banking family. The effect of the newcomers on the farming landscape can be illustrated by the activities of another settler by Derwentwater,

99

Lord William Gordon. Perhaps in a desire to distance himself from London, where the anti-Catholic 'Gordon Riots' of 1780, led by his brother, had tarnished the family name, Lord William made enquiries in 1781 about buying an estate at Waterend, on the west bank of Derwentwater, belonging to a yeoman called John Fletcher. Over the next four years he bought up the whole of the western shore of the lake from Faw Park to Manesty. He replaced the farm at Waterend with Derwent Bay House; built a house at Silver Hill and was instrumental in re-routing the road from Portinscale to Borrowdale higher up the hillside away from his new retreat in the late 1780s. The farms along the western bank of Derwentwater had contained considerable acreages of old coppice woodland before Lord William bought them but this had recently been felled. He replanted it with a variety of species: oak, spruce, silver fir, Weymouth pine and larch. The woods on the north side of Derwent Bay House were criss-crossed by gravelled drives and footpaths, the effect being to create a landscape 'all trimly kept, and yet free from anything to mar its rural beauty'. His aim was to enhance the natural beauty of fellside and water by planting parts with woodland to create an idealised image of mountain scenery.

Beside Windermere the planting of lakeside estates was carried out with more of an eye to commercial forestry. Bishop Watson, who planted Gummer's How with larch in 1805–6, and John Christian Curwen, who clothed Claife Heights with larch and oak between 1798 and 1802, were both agricultural improvers who saw their plantations as expressions of the spirit of scientific farming.

The Age of Improvement thus generated considerable change in the farming landscape of the Lake District. The stimulus was both economic improvement, in the case of Parliamentary Enclosure, and aesthetic improvement, in the pursuit of the picturesque. Most valleys contain elements inherited from this period, either adding to or replacing parts of the countryside known to the 'statesmen. The landscape which Lake District lovers have sought to preserve since the 1880s is thus the product of centuries of change. It was and remains largely a landscape created by farming and, as such, is a dynamic, living complex which will continue to change in response to variations in the way the land of valley and fellside is managed by man.

5
THE INDUSTRIAL
LANDSCAPE

IT is not by chance that some of the most attractive parts of the country have a long industrial history. The Lake District is no exception. Features which make up the distinctive scenery have themselves either formed the basis of industrial activities or are the product of a well developed rural economy. These basic features – rock, woodland and water – are typical of the Lake District landscape. Let us examine the patterns, colours and textures formed by these features and look into and interpret this working landscape.

Over the centuries, very little has been written down or recorded about everyday life and occupations, yet the surviving relics have so much to tell us about local life and the industrial landscape. In the Lake District, between the late medieval times and the mid nineteenth century, it was common to find a virtually self-sufficient local economy with its wide range of local occupations and services. At the same time certain industries of regional and even national importance were developed. Local place-names are synonymous with industry such as Furness Iron; Whitehaven Coal; Honister Slate; Coniston Copper; Shap Granite; Keswick Pencils and Kendal Green cloth. Most industry was to be found in rural locations, relying on a scattered population and related to the availability of resources, fuel and power, rather than in urban centres.

ROCKS

Rock has long been used as a building material and the surface expression of the underlying geology is seen in the field walls and local buildings. Because of the difficulties in transporting heavy stone over a rugged landscape in the seventeenth and eighteenth centuries, it was necessary to have a scatter of small quarries supplying stone for building walls, bridges, farm buildings and houses. Most of these early

101

Plate 24 The Tilberthwaite area contains extensive remains and features of the slate quarrying industry *(Andrew Lowe)*

workings have now blended into the landscape.

In the heart of the Lake District the Borrowdale Volcanic rocks have two main bands which possess exceptionally good cleavage, enabling the rock to be split into slates. At the northern band, Honister Quarry high on the fells between Borrowdale and Buttermere began working on a more substantial scale during the late seventeenth century in response to the new demands for rebuilding the medieval farmsteads in stone. The southern band runs between the Duddon Valley and Shap, and by the late eighteenth century quarries in the Torver, Coniston, Tilberthwaite and Langdale area were well established (Plate 24). The industrial revolution brought a dramatic increase in demand for roofing slate to cover the thousands of town houses. This was accompanied by technological developments in transport, initially with roads and canals, but especially with the railways during the mid nineteenth century and consequently the peak production for slate quarrying came in the 1890s. These new demands required a slate of consistent quality much thinner and more regular than the old slate flags. This had the advantage of easier carting and transport, as well as covering more roof area per ton. Quarries were developed in relatively remote locations where the main bands of slate were cut across by valleys, such as Borrowdale, Longsleddale, Kentmere, Troutbeck,

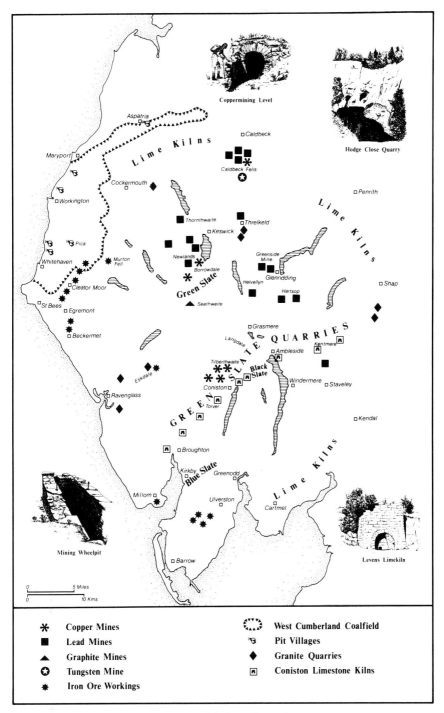

Coppermining Level

Hodge Close Quarry

Mining Wheelpit

Levens Limekiln

✳	Copper Mines
■	Lead Mines
▲	Graphite Mines
✪	Tungsten Mine
❋	Iron Ore Workings

🌀	West Cumberland Coalfield
ꙮ	Pit Villages
◆	Granite Quarries
▣	Coniston Limestone Kilns

Fig 17 Wealth from the rocks

Kirkstone and Langdale. Consequently slate quarrying has left behind a rich legacy of remote and high level workings providing strong visual evidence of past industry.

The best quality slate lies well below the ground surface. To reach it, the quarrymen set to work on the valley side by drilling, blasting and chiselling tunnels or levels into the fellside. It was common practice to work along the cleavage or 'bate' of the rock and follow the slate vein in a series of steps. The waste heaps stepping up the fellside are traditional Lakeland features and later workings sometimes opened up a long cleft in the landscape, as at Penny Rigg Quarry, Tilberthwaite. Underground, manageable blocks or 'clogs' of slate could be carefully extracted using gunpowder. Left behind were huge caverns or 'close-heads'. In areas such as Tilberthwaite or on Loughrigg Terrace, near Rydal, few visitors can fail to be impressed by the scale of these man-made caverns. The blocks of slate were pushed on flat tramway bogeys out of the levels to the dressing sheds. Here, the skilled 'rivers' and 'dressers' split and trimmed the roofing slate to its familiar shape. Slates were carefully packed into wooden crates or boxes and transported to the markets by a variety of means including packhorses, horse and sled, carts, lake craft, canal barges and railway wagons. Extraction, processing, transport and the quarryman's way of life have left behind the tell-tale evidence and clues. At the old quarry face, the signs of split-open drill holes, and nearby ruined buildings, rusting wagon wheels and twisted rails, remind us of more prosperous times. Quarry names such as Klondyke and Spion Kop take us back to the pioneering days of Victorian times when slate had to be 'won'. There is plenty of visible evidence of the quarrymen's communities. A good example is the isolated cluster of buildings at Hodge Close, Tilberthwaite.

Older slate quarries add scale, colour and textures to relatively isolated areas, reminding us that the Lake District has been and still is a living, working landscape. The thin sheets and flakes of waste slate vary in colour from dull greens to shades of grey, darkened with the passing years. Each quarrying area or even a single quarry face varies in its colour and texture of slate, as well as its quality and suitability for splitting. Near the head of the Kentmere Valley the slate is steel-grey with a distinct sheen; light sea green is found at Kirkstone, Elterwater and Borrowdale; olive green at Honister and Moss Rigg, Tilberthwaite; blue and blue-grey at Kirkby-in-Furness and blue-black at Brathay near Ambleside.

South of the main geological division lie extensive areas of Silurian rocks, made up of sedimentary gritstones, flagstones and shales. The most productive were the Brathay Flags, which were worked for blue-black roofing slate at Brathay and Kirkby-in-Furness at the famous Burlington Quarries. Here the largest slate quarry in the Lake District, under the control of the Earl of Burlington, began production of roofing slate on a large scale after the 1840s. Although the vast workings are hidden from view, the extensive waste heaps along the hillside facing the Duddon Estuary form very prominent landscape features and reveal the scale of 150 years of continuous working (Fig 18). Unlike the green slate, these blue slate quarries were generally worked on opencast methods. Elsewhere in the Silurian formations numerous abandoned roadside quarries are scattered over the southern Lake District. Because the cleavage was not good enough for roofing slate and the rock fractured at awkward angles, these quarries produced rough walling stone and roadstone.

Limestone and granite are contrasting minerals in terms of colour, texture and past uses, yet in recent years both have been quarried for use in road construction. Around the Lake District is an outer ring of Carboniferous Limestone, giving rise to a very distinctive landscape of grey and white outcrops, linear patterns of neat stone walls, attractive villages, good quality pastures and native woodlands clinging to the steep slopes. Where limestone contained numerous fossils, its attractive qualities were revealed by polishing to give the effect of marble. Kendal, known as the 'auld grey town' because of the widespread use of limestone in its buildings, was also a centre of 'marble' production in the nineteenth century. At Scout Scar, Kendal and at Whitbarrow, near the Lyth Valley, the limestone lies in thick, even beds making it ideal for cutting and dressing into large runner stones for the gunpowder mills. Identifying abandoned limestone quarries can be difficult as they soon become assimilated into the landscape.

Neatly built lime kilns provide further evidence of industrial activity in the limestone landscape. These small furnaces used wood, peat, charcoal or coal as layers of fuel to roast small lumps of limestone and produce pure lime. There were two main uses of lime – to act as a fertilizer on the more acid soils of the Lake District and to be slaked with water for making building mortar, the protective roughcast for the farmhouses and the traditional limewash. The majority of kilns are found on the Carboniferous Limestone, but a few examples are still to be seen on a narrow band of poor quality Coniston Limestone which runs parallel to the main geological division between Shap and Millom. Stockdale kiln, in the Longsleddale Valley and Yewdale kiln, just north of Coniston are good examples, probably dating from the late eighteenth century and built of local slate stone.

On Carboniferous Limestone, the kilns are generally built of neatly

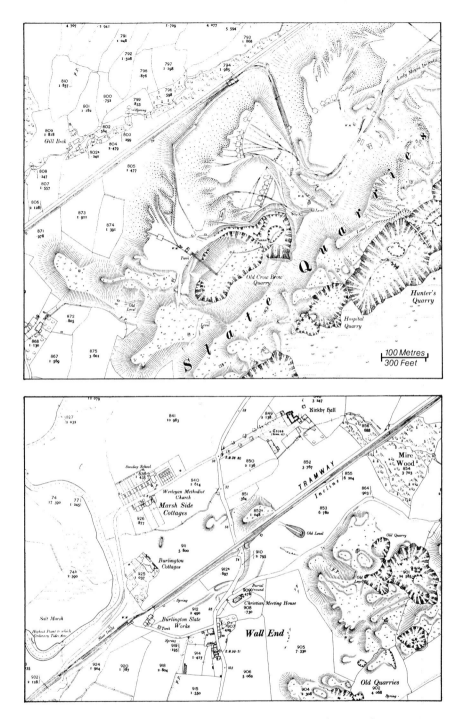

Fig 18 A landscape of slate: Kirkby-in-Furness. Extracts from Ordnance Survey 1:2500 scale map, published 1913.

dressed blocks of limestone with the furnace linings made of firebrick. They were sited near a quarry, not far from the trade routes and often in prominent, exposed positions to take advantage of a natural draught to sustain the firing process. Travellers along the A590, just west of Levens Bridge, will notice the small field kiln, attractively set against a limestone outcrop. Nearby, at Whitbarrow, also to the west of Kendal and around Cartmel are good examples which were encouraged by the opening of the Lancaster to Kendal Canal in 1819. This enabled the easy transport of bulky lime to the Lancashire towns and agricultural areas. In the northern Lake District, both small field kilns for farmers' use and larger commercial kilns are visible near Shap, Penrith, Caldbeck and Cockermouth. The distribution pattern of limekilns therefore pinpoints quite accurately the outline of the underlying geology and provides industrial relics in an otherwise agricultural landscape (see Fig 17).

Granite intrusions appear to burst through the surface geology of the Lake District. As the rock solidified and crystallised at different rates, so each area developed its own distinctive type of granite. Granite varies from the course grained pink at Shap, to the mottled pink, white and grey at Eskdale and Ennerdale. At Threlkeld the micro-granite is a fine grained green/grey rock, and at the Shap 'blue' quarry the rock is a blue/grey containing garnets. Small granite quarries were opened up in the seventeenth and eighteenth centuries, in response to the phase of rebuilding, to supply roughly dressed granite blocks for constructing farmhouses, barns and bridges. Later, during the nineteenth century came the urban demands for setts, kerbs, roadstone and concrete paving flags. Quarries which were able to take advantage of the railways and by developing mineral tramways, soon expanded on a considerable scale. Prominent examples of such quarries can be seen at Shap, Threlkeld and Embleton, with smaller ones in Eskdale. When polished, the Shap pink granite is a very attractive and unique ornamental stone.

As with the limestone workings, granite quarries soon become well vegetated when abandoned. A good example is at Beckfoot in Eskdale which was served by the Ravenglass and Eskdale narrow gauge railway. In less than thirty years since the quarry was in active operation, the site is now an attractive overgrown feature, recently designated as a site of special scientific interest. As a complete contrast, in the more open landscape of the west-facing fellside between Threlkeld Quarry and the Vale of St John, a series of old quarries strung out along an old mineral line appear to have been gouged out by a huge scoop. Granite quarrying has left behind a varied legacy of landscape features, the most apparent being the craggy rock faces, sometimes glistening with quartz and other minerals. In addition, fine waste heaps from the hand dressings; the remains of the crushing equipment; concrete, stone and brick structures; engine houses; tramway inclines and well engineered mineral railways complete the picture.

Although these physical remains give an impression of the scale and former importance of past quarrying activities, the quarryworkers' houses and industrial communities tell us that there is a human story behind the gaunt ruins. At Threlkeld, close to the site of the old station on the Penrith to Keswick railway, are rows of well-built industrial houses, which were once supported by a chapel, school and meeting room. Shap developed as a seventeenth-century market town on the trade route to Scotland, but after the railway opened to Carlisle in 1846, it became an important centre of granite and limestone quarrying. Today, these industries still dominate the landscape and are the mainstay of the local economy.

The distinctive character of buildings in the vicinity of Penrith and along the coastal strip between St Bees and the Furness peninsula, is the result of locally quarried red sandstone. It was machine sawed or hand dressed into blocks, slabs, steps, window surrounds, quoins and lintels, or used as decorative features for important religious buildings. In contrast to the prominent spoil heaps of the slate workings, the old sandstone quarries have blended into the landscape.

Although there are no coal reserves within the National Park, in an area between Whitehaven, Workington, Maryport and Aspatria there is evidence of coal mining since the seventeenth century. Whitehaven's prosperity in the eighteenth century was the result of successful coal-mining activity and commerce in the hands of the influential Lowther family. This coalfield was the industrial foundation of West Cumberland. Deep mining reached its peak in the early twentieth century, but 1986 marked the end of an important era when Haig Pit, Whitehaven closed. The typical surface features, common to all coalmining areas, such as the pit head gear, shale heaps and mineral railways are becoming more of a rarity in the 1980s. Overlooking Whitehaven harbour the prominent 'candlestick' chimney of Wellington Pit, dating from the 1840s, is a well known landmark. The nearby pit head buildings at Saltom Pit and the castellated turrets and ornate engine house at Jane Pit, Workington, are fine, industrial features. Coalmining landscapes contain strong reminders of the miner's life, as with the pit villages of Siddick, Lowca, Parton and Flimby strung along the coastal fringe, and Harriston near Aspatria. Pica, with the very long terraces, is one of the smallest, yet most conspicuous mining communities, occupying a windswept skyline position in an open landscape between Workington and Whitehaven. Large-scale opencast workings began in the 1950s, by excavating the coal seam to depths of up to 300ft (90m), using huge draglines. Subsequent regrading and restoration work has created a new landscape. Although the end result is an improvement in agricultural terms, the landscape loses its farms and field boundaries, as well as the relics of past industries. Only one of the classic coned shaped colliery heaps survives, at Dearham Bridge, to the north-east of Maryport. It lies within an attractive section of the Ellen Valley and should perhaps be retained as a monument to the coalmining industry.

The Lake District rocks contain a wealth of minerals including copper, lead and iron, with even small quantities of gold and silver. Almost every valley and fell of the Lake District shows signs of mining activities, whether as initial prospecting trial levels or as successful enterprises. Men had to win these minerals in a harsh climate on the surface and even more hazardous conditions underground. Initially a mineral vein was worked from the surface by chiselling at the extremely hard quartz to remove the metal bearing ore, leaving behind a narrow cleft in the landscape. Levels were also driven into the hillside to reach the veins, and unlike the wide slate levels, these entrances and passages were narrow and beautifully shaped to serve three main functions – access, drainage and ventilation.

Attractive stone arched levels are common features in the mining areas, mostly dating from the early to mid nineteenth century. As workings progressed deeper, vertical shafts were excavated, often well over 1,000ft (300m) below the surface, to link with the maze of underground levels. The sequence of processes in extracting, sorting, the use of water power and methods of transport means that old mining sites have a great variety of interesting industrial features. Together, they make a significant contribution to landscape character.

The story of the German miners coming to Keswick and Coniston in Elizabethan times has been well told. These miners were employed by the Company of the Mines Royal to exploit the mineral wealth of the Lake District. During the latter part of the sixteenth century and until the mid-seventeenth century, the men from Augsburg established the Lake District as an important centre of copper mining and smelting. At Brigham beside the River Greta were some of the largest copper smelters in Europe. The greatest period of prosperity for the Coniston Coppermines was between the 1830s and 1860s when John Taylor and John Barratt came from Cornwall with Cornish experience, technology, finance and the vital ingredient – Cornishmen. Most of the remains to be seen today in the Coppermines Valley date from this

Plate 25 Coniston Coppermines Valley shows considerable evidence of mining activities, set in a dramatic, rugged landscape *(Andrew Lowe)*

period with numerous levels, shafts, waterwheel pits, mill races, tramways, ruined buildings and extensive waste heaps. At the height of production during the late 1850s perhaps as many as 600 men, women and children were employed at the Coniston mines producing 250 tons of copper per month. Individually, the surviving features are important relics of industrial archaeology, but collectively they form an industrial historic landscape now given official recognition as a scheduled ancient monument (Plate 25).

Copper is a difficult mineral to smelt, and the English Copper Company developed Swansea as the main smelting centre for Britain, with St Helens serving north-west England. So the prosperity of Lake District copper mines depended on efficient transport to these smelters. In the early nineteenth century, the route from the Coniston mines to the smelters involved horse and cart to the quay, lake craft on Coniston Water, storage at High Nibthwaite, horse and cart to Greenodd and then coastal craft. The Coniston Coppermining Company was therefore anxious to promote a railway link, which eventually reached Coniston Village in 1859. After intermittent activity in the 1880s, and the early twentieth century, the mines were no longer worked commercially after World War I.

Quartz veins also contain lead ore and the working of this valuable mineral has left behind unmistakable marks on the landscape. In contrast to the brown stained copper heaps, lead mining waste is grey, white and toxic and very few plants are able to tolerate it. Early lead mines were worked in the Newlands Valley by the German miners of the Mines Royal Company, but the main period of activity came in the mid to late nineteenth century in response to the urban demands for lead piping, water tanks and sheet lead for roofs. Productive veins of lead occurred within the Skiddaw Slates in the Caldbeck Fells, Keswick and Newlands Valley areas and within the Borrowdale Volcanic rocks in the Helvellyn Fells. Smaller workings are still visible in the more lowland areas, for example to the north of Staveley near Kendal within the Silurian rock formations. The German miners established their main lead smelter at Stoneycroft, to the south-west of Keswick, in the 1560s, but the visible remains date mainly from the early nineteenth century. North of Kirkstone Pass near Hartsop Hall are the remains of an eighteenth-century smelter owned by the National Trust and protected as a scheduled ancient monument. During the nineteenth century, as with copper, lead smelting furnaces became more specialised, with large-scale operations at Newcastle upon Tyne and in South Wales.

Techniques of lead ore extraction were very similar to copper mining sites. Apart from the typical mine features of water leats, wheelpits, dressing floors, stone buildings and structures, it is the unvegetated lead waste heaps which stand out so clearly in the Lakeland landscape. In the Caldbeck Fells, the Potts Ghyll, Sandbeds, Driggeth and Roughten Gill mines are still important features within a rather desolate fell landscape, even though some reclamation of derelict pylons, gantries and corrugated iron buildings took place in the 1960s. It is ironic that the successful mining operations often end up with the poorest display of old features. They are either swept away during generations of modernisation, or are finally dismantled upon closure. There is a fine dividing line between derelict eyesores and relics of our industrial heritage.

In the Keswick area, the remains of Gategill mine at Threlkeld, Brandlehow mines near Derwentwater and on the adjacent Cat Bells ridge are prominent beside popular fell paths. The 'witches hand' stretching down the fell above the Barrow mine in the lower Newlands Valley illustrates the effect of steep slopes and toxic lead waste. Between Helvellyn and Glenridding, the Greenside mine was one of the most important lead mines in Britain. Here, the galena contained 12oz (300grms) of silver per ton of lead and it was refined during the smelting process. By Lakeland and national standards it was a pioneering mine, being the first metal mine in Britain to introduce electric locomotives in 1893 and electric winding equipment in 1896.

Although most Lake District mines closed by the early twentieth century, Greenside mine continued until 1962; consequently, there is a range of evidence spanning three centuries. The oldest workings from the eighteenth century appear as collapsed gashes on the fellside at 2,000ft (600m) above sea level, with the extensive operations of the 1820s and 1830s on a level area at 1,800ft (550m). Here are the long fingers of coarse waste – straight from the mine – with smooth mounds of fine waste from the dressing floors. To complete the scene there is an old lagoon with a breached dam, ruined wheelpits, water leats, tramways, stone foundations, ore crushers and cobbled floors. Lower down an old incline tramway plunges down the steep valley side and a nineteenth-century chimney flue winds its way up through the landscape for 2 kilometres. Large-scale working in the twentieth century has left behind two massive tailings dams of fine toxic waste. Greenside mine not only had a visually dominating effect on the valley, but it had a social impact and Glenridding village is a fine example of a miners' community with rows of stone terraced houses down the valley.

Of all the Lake District minerals, iron ore is the most colourful. It colours the ground, excavations, paths, tracks and old buildings. The rounded nodules of iron resemble kidneys in colour and shape. Haematite deposits occur in various rocks, including Carboniferous Limestone, Granite, Skiddaw Slates and Borrowdale Volcanics. In the limestone areas of Egremont, Cleator Moor, Millom and Lindal-in-Furness the iron lay in cavities as huge horizontal deposits. These varied in thickness from one metre to 250ft (75m). In some cases the deposits have been worked as open quarries, but the majority of workings were underground leaving behind very extensive areas of caverns. Later subsidence gives the appearance of a collapsed landscape. The most productive area of West Cumberland lay along a narrow strip between Beckermet, Egremont, Moor Row, Cleator Moor, Frizington and Arlecdon. This iron-based industrial landscape makes a very strong visual statement, with red stained soil and spoil heaps, derelict buildings, sinuous mineral railways and long rows of workers houses. Overall, this strikes quite a discordant note in an otherwise rural scene, particularly with a magnificent backcloth of the Ennerdale Fells. The dramatic impact on the landscape was essentially a product of the Victorian age, with early mining in the 1840s stimulated by the demands of the new Bessemer steel making process and assisted by the railway links between mines, works and ports.

Iron had been mined on a small scale near Millom in the seventeenth century for local smelting, but large-scale workings of the famous Hodbarrow mines began in the 1860s and continued until 1968. Massive ore deposits lay under the Duddon Estuary and to reach these safely, large coastal barriers were built in the 1880s, with the final outer barrier completed in 1905. It is a credit to the builders that this great feat of civil engineering still serves its purpose today. As in West Cumbria, the story of iron is written clearly in the landscape, especially the town of Millom – a creation of Victorian prosperity.

Away from these more obvious industrial landscapes, there are still distinct traces of iron mining within the National Park area. At Murton Fell, to the north of Ennerdale, the old mineral railway is the vital clue to trace across the landscape. Other tell-tale clues are the local place-names, which describe the natural outcrops of haematite. Red Gill, Red Screes and Ore Gap are names well known to fellwalkers. In the heart of the Lake District rich haematite veins were worked near Red Tarn, opposite the Langdale Pikes and on the west-facing slopes of Fairfield near Grasmere between the seventeenth and early nineteenth centuries. A closer look at the buildings of Grasmere village reveals widespread iron staining on the green volcanic rocks.

On the fellside near Seathwaite in Borrowdale the dark grey spoil heaps identify the famous graphite or black lead mines, which were opened in Elizabethan times and later supported both a small cottage industry and pencil factories. Cumberland pencils are still made today using imported graphite. In the Carrock Fell area, at the head of the Mosedale Valley another rare mineral is found – wolfram, the ore of tungsten. The Carrock mine worked intermittently during the nineteenth and twentieth centuries to supply tungsten for use in specialised steels.

WOODLANDS

While rocks form the basic shape of the Lake District fells, the local landscape character of the dales is enhanced by the trees and woodlands. It seems hard to believe that these quiet woodlands, today left to nature and a few deer, were once thriving centres of crafts and industries. Over the country as a whole it is the areas which have had a long history of woodland management to support rural industries, which retain a wooded legacy. For example parts of Scotland, South Yorkshire, Shropshire, Forest of Dean, the Weald and of course the Lake District all have attractive wooded areas. In the Lake District the

Plate 26 A drive up the Rusland Valley past the famous beeches is an ideal way to appreciate the landscape importance of old coppice woodlands *(Andrew Lowe)*

old coppice woodlands are to be found principally in the High Furness area where there is one of the most extensive areas of deciduous woodland in Britain. This area contains the Rusland Valley (Plate 26), Coniston and Crake Valleys and Skelwith, whilst other notable woods are in the Windermere area, near Grasmere and Rydal, Winster Valley, Duddon Valley, Eskdale, Borrowdale and near Ullswater (Fig 19).

The woodlands were a living resource and, until fairly recent times, were also a resource where woodmen and their families earned a living. These deciduous woods consisted basically of oak, ash, beech, birch, hazel, sycamore and alder, together with the evergreen holly, pine and yew. Out of these woods came a variety of raw materials, including timber, coppice wood, brushwood and bark, for use in long established rural crafts. Oak trees have traditionally supplied durable timber for building ships and houses, ash for use as oars and tool handles, birch for wood turning and besom brushes, hazel for withies and laths, and alder for clog soles.

In the Lake District the most important resource was coppice wood. A young tree was 'coppiced' by cutting it down about 1ft (30cm) above the ground, so that in Spring it would send up a group of shoots from the stumps (or stools). Each shoot competes for light and after about

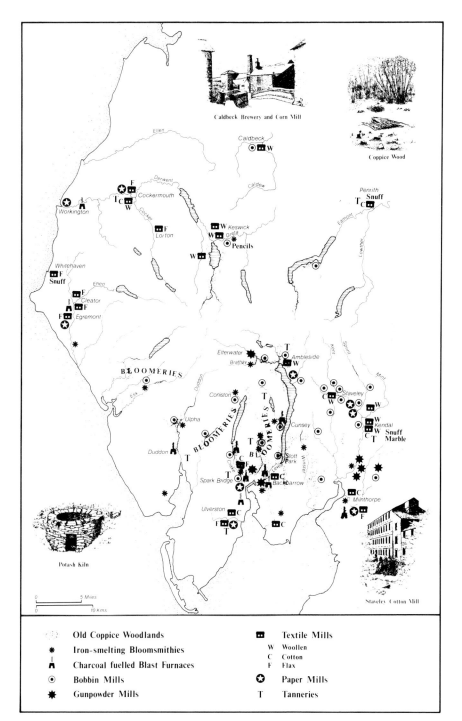

Caldbeck Brewery and Corn Mill

Coppice Wood

Potash Kiln

Staveley Cotton Mill

⣿ Old Coppice Woodlands	⬛ Textile Mills
✳ Iron-smelting Bloomsmithies	W Woollen
	C Cotton
♙ Charcoal fuelled Blast Furnaces	F Flax
⊙ Bobbin Mills	✪ Paper Mills
✴ Gunpowder Mills	T Tanneries

Fig 19 Water power and woodlands

fifteen years the coppice consists of up to 20 poles, about 5in (12cm) thick and 20ft (6m) long. By regular coppicing, the tree would be cropped and the root system invigorated. A well managed coppice wood could supply raw materials and products for smelting, tanning, brewing, mining, quarrying, textiles, agriculture, shipping, road transport, as well as the construction of houses, furniture, mills and mill machinery.

Although the woodland industries have left a wealth of evidence, we have to look closely within or near the woods to pick out the features and clues. Grouped alongside old woodland tracks can be seen circular clearings or platforms about 20ft (6m) in diameter. These are the 'pitsteads', the relics of a once famous charcoal burning industry which began originally with the monks of Furness Abbey providing charcoal to smelt iron. In essence, the object was to char a stack of coppice wood by slow burning and about 5 tons of wood produced about 1 ton of charcoal. This process lasted between 3 and 5 days, requiring continuous supervision by the colliers, who lived next to the burn in wigwam-style huts made of branches with a turf weatherproof covering. By the twentieth century charcoal burning was dying out and the last traditional burn took place near Backbarrow in 1937.

Charcoal was a vital fuel for industrial purposes such as glass-making, potteries, bakeries and blacksmiths as well as domestic uses, but its main use was to smelt iron. Early smelting hearths were known as 'bloomeries' operated since the Iron Age and Roman times until the late Middle Ages. These were set up into the woodlands as it was more economical to transport the rich iron ore than the bulky charcoal. Bloomeries had hand or foot operated bellows for blowing air into a stone and clay miniature furnace to produce small 'blooms' of iron. By heating and hammering, excellent quality wrought iron was produced, leaving behind large heaps of slaggy materials. These are the vital clues for identifying bloomery sites as well as local names such as Cinder Hill, Forge Wood and Smithy Beck. Although they are found scattered over a wide area of the Lake District, the main concentrations are in High Furness and Eskdale – both are close to haematite deposits and extensive coppice woodlands. Later, in the sixteenth century, water power was harnessed to power leather bellows and to operate trip or tilt hammers. These more durable stone-built furnaces were known as 'bloomsmithies'.

The slag was collected in a rounded depression and so formed pillow-shaped pieces known locally as 'mossers'. As they make ideal cam stones for wall tops, many can be seen in the Crake Valley between Nibthwaite and Penny Bridge. Small industrial communities were named after these iron workings, the most expressive being Spark Bridge, in the Crake Valley. Bloomsmithies continued to smelt ore successfully into the early eighteenth century at sites such as Coniston, Little Langdale, Winster Valley, Rusland Valley, Cartmel, Backbarrow, Milnthorpe and Eskdale.

The year 1711 marked a major breakthrough in the local technology for smelting iron. Although the blast furnace had been introduced from the continent into Sussex in the late fifteenth century, the bloomery method produced sufficient quantities of good quality iron. With the increase in population, and development of other rural industries, the demand for iron tools and implements increased; and blast furnaces were introduced into the Furness area of the Lake District. This area possessed all the requirements – extensive charcoal coppice woodland, rich local supplies of iron ore and plentiful sources of water to power huge bellows. Between 1711 and 1748 charcoal-fired blast furnaces were set up at Backbarrow, Cunsey, Leighton (south of Milnthorpe) Nibthwaite, Duddon Bridge, Low Wood and Penny Bridge. These furnaces used up vast quantities of coppice woodland, for each furnace produced between 10 and 15 tons of cast iron per week, requiring on average one acre of coppice per ton of iron.

Remains of these blast furnaces are the most impressive, functional, yet attractive features of rural industry. Only Backbarrow Furnace survived through into the twentieth century and after converting to coke fuel in 1926, it finally ceased in 1966. Most of the other furnace sites have some remains visible, but a little imagination and careful searching is needed. Later industrial uses, natural decay, deliberate destruction and vegetation growth have made the task more difficult. However, the Duddon Iron Furnace, dating from 1736 with its magnificent stone-built furnace stack, huge stores for charcoal and iron ore and the remains of the iron workers cottages, is the most complete charcoal blast furnace still surviving in England (Plate 27). It is protected as a scheduled ancient monument and is being looked after by the National Park Authority. Adjoining the site is Furnace Wood with its evidence of coppicing and pitsteads. The furnace closed down in 1867 by which time coke had become well established as the main fuel to smelt iron. No longer were the woodlands of the Lake District the main attraction for iron smelting, for the orefields, the coalfields and the railways became the key factors.

Thus the iron smelting industry migrated out of the southern Lake District, especially with the development of the Bessemer steel process after 1856 which suited the Cumberland and Furness haematite. Steam-powered blast furnaces were soon set up in the Workington,

Plate 27 Duddon Iron Furnace is an impressive structure built in 1737 to smelt Furness iron ore using the local supplies of charcoal *(Simon Kent)*

Millom and Barrow areas leading to major urban developments with typical Victorian planning and architecture. In the 1880s at the height of prosperity there were fifty-four blast furnaces in production in West Cumberland alone.

In iron making, charcoal was used as a fuel, but it also formed the vital ingredient for a substance in great demand by the mines and quarries – gunpowder. The best charcoal for gunpowder production was obtained from alder and juniper. Its use was first recorded in the mines and quarries in the late seventeenth century, but the industry did not start in the Lake District until 1764, when John Wakefield of Kendal built the Sedgwick Works. By the mid nineteenth century powder mills were operating also at Gatebeck, Low Wood (near Haverthwaite), Elterwater and Black Beck (near Bouth). These mills required very large, often linear sites so that buildings could be kept apart to prevent the knock-on effect of explosions, but also necessitated the use of elaborate horse-drawn tramway systems. Mills were sited near the estuaries of Morecambe Bay, or existing trade routes, for the import of Chilean saltpetre and sulphur from Stromboli, and near good supplies of water power. The ingredients had to be carefully ground together or

118

'incorporated' and then passed through a series of processes to produce a consistent quality and grain size of black powder. By 1937 all the works had closed down due to the increasing use of chemical explosives. Today most gunpowder mill sites still retain some features, including large runner stones, wheelpits, water races, blast walls, overgrown tramways and thickly wooded blast screens. The Langdale timeshare development occupies the site of the Elterwater Gunpowder works, whilst some of the others have become caravan sites. As time passes and the trees cover yet more remains it becomes increasingly difficult to visualise that these sites were once some of the most extensive and labour-intensive industrial mills in the Lake District.

Besides these large-scale industries, the woodlands supported a variety of crafts, in particular the making of 'swill' (or spelk) baskets. These coracle-shaped baskets, made from thin pieces of split oak woven on a hazel frame, were produced locally since early medieval times. In the nineteenth century almost every village in the southern Lake District had its swiller, with places such as Broughton-in-Furness and Lowick the important centres. Sadly, today this skilled craft has virtually died out. The 'swilling shops' are difficult to identify, many have been converted or demolished and the once common iron boiling tank, about 10-12ft (3m) long, is hard to find.

Most coppice was cut in autumn, but oak was usually left until May or June when the sap was rising and the bark could be peeled off. In the woods are circular or oval-shaped low stone walls with a hearth which formed the basis of a bark peeler's hut. Here lived the peeler with his family who were also engaged in occupations such as making besoms, clothespegs or tent pegs. Oak bark was sent from the woods to the local tanneries. Of all the products to come out of the woods, for each acre the bark was the most valuable. Tanneries were established in most urban centres, but the industry was concentrated in the High Furness area at Ambleside, Hawkshead, Coniston, Rusland, Lowick, Penny Bridge, Greenodd, Broughton, Ulverston and especially at Kendal, still famous for its shoes. The introduction of chemical tanning using chromium salts, in the mid nineteenth century, led to the closure of most rural tanneries. A few buildings survive, a good example being the Rusland Tannery near Rusland Hall, but others are merely ruins or filled-in pits. Old maps contain the hidden clues with names such as Bark House, Bark Booth, Tanyard Cottage, Tanpit Lane and Tanner's Wood.

A walk through old coppices may reveal masonry-lined pits or stone-built kilns, about 12ft (3-4m) in diameter set against sloping ground. These are the late medieval relics of a potash burning industry.

Green twigs and bracken were burnt in these kilns so it is common to find these attractive structures in open landscapes as well as within woodlands. Potash formed an essential ingredient for producing soft soaps to help wash the local fleeces as part of the Kendal woollen industry. Over two hundred kilns have been identified in the Lake District and adjoining areas. Some of the kilns are larger, about 15ft (5m) in diameter, and as these occur near lead mines, they were probably 'kilnwood' kilns for producing the kiln-dried timber or 'white coals' to fuel the lead smelters in the seventeenth and eighteenth centuries. A particularly fine example is at Elfhowe, to the north of Staveley, near Kendal. As with other woodland crafts and industries, old maps reveal a host of place-name evidence such as Kiln Bank, Kilner Coppice, Hellpot Wood, Ashes, Ashburner Side and Ealinghearth.

Since medieval times, the Lake District had its turners producing cups, platters and dishes from birch and sycamore. This rural craft became a famous large-scale industry with the rise of the Lancashire cotton industry in the late eighteenth century. Steam-powered cotton

Plate 28 Dating from 1835, Stott Park Bobbin Mill used water power and later steam power to drive lathes for turning bobbins from coppice wood. It is now open as a fascinating industrial museum (*Andrew Lowe*)

spinning mills required millions of wooden reels and bobbins. Between the 1790s and 1860 over 60 bobbin mills were established in the Lake District, mainly in the High Furness area, but as far afield as Caldbeck, Keswick, Eskdale and Howtown. A few were purpose-built mills, but the majority were adapted from other uses, in particular redundant iron furnaces, woollen mills and corn mills. The mills used mainly birch and sycamore, although beech produced smooth centres for large reels and ash, being an elastic wood, was ideally suited for making tool handles and oars. Bobbins were turned on cast iron lathes made locally by Fell at Troutbeck Bridge near Windermere or Braithwaite at Crook. Bobbin making was a labour-intensive industry and the working conditions continued unchanged well into the mid twentieth century. Staveley near Kendal became the centre of the bobbin turning industry and today the Staveley Woodturning Company still produces turned tool handles.

The decline of the Lancashire cotton industry, the introduction of mass-produced plastic bobbins and reels in the twentieth century, ultimately led to the eclipse of this well known Lakeland industry. Only Stott Park Bobbin Mill, to the north of Newby Bridge, dating from 1835 and working until 1971 is now open in the summer months as an excellent industrial museum (Plate 28).

WATER

Finally, in order to draw together all the various aspects of the industrial landscapes with a common thread, it is worthwhile to examine water as a vital provider of power. Rivers, streams, tarns and lakes help to give the Lake District its distinctive character. When other areas abandoned water power in favour of steam power, the Lake District continued to rely on it well into the twentieth century.

Within the fells, Lake District mining industry was dependent on water power for lifting the ore out of the mines, for driving the crushers and for powering the pumps. Within remote areas some of the largest waterwheels in England were to be found in the mid nineteenth century. To ensure a regular supply of water, elaborate water courses were engineered, running down the valley sides or crossing from one valley to another, a good lesson in water conservation. Fine examples are visible in the upper part of the Coniston Coppermines Valley dating from the 1830s to the 1850s. Within the mining areas the surviving relics show a high degree of skill and ingenuity, from the massive stone dams holding back vast quantities of water, to the masonry-lined mill races and the neatly built, functional wheelpits. At altitudes well over 1,000ft (300m), one can but marvel at the quality and precision of the massive slate block walls, still surviving long after other buildings and structures have disappeared.

In the more lowland areas no complete waterwheels survive at the old iron working sites, although the bloomsmithies, furnaces and forges were so dependent on water power for operating bellows and hammers. As with the mining sites, the iron industry required a slow axle speed and a constant supply of water for many weeks once a furnace began in blast. Evidence of 'hammer' ponds and mill races can be traced, but within the wooded valleys the vegetation growth makes identification difficult. At the Duddon Furnace the water was channelled through the woods from the River Duddon for over ¹/₂ mile, to turn a low breast 27ft (8.5m) diameter wheel. During excavations in 1983 the remains of a wheel were found, preserved in the thick black mud. It dated from the 1820s and was made of pinewood with iron strappings, bolts and connecting plates. During the archaeological dig it was apparent that there had been at least three different sized wheels operating between 1738 and 1867.

Although the low axle speeds were needed for the mines and iron working sites, the bobbin mills used narrow lightly built wheels, geared up to drive line shafting and high speed lathes. At Stott Park the mill was originally powered in the late 1830s by a 32ft (10m) diameter wheel which was later replaced by turbines, a steam engine and finally electric motors. The main reservoir of water for the mill is nearby at High Dam, a popular picnic area with its old charcoal coppices and larch trees. Few visitors realise that this attractive tarn is an industrial relic.

The manufacture of gunpowder made heavy demands on water power with complex systems of millraces. As described earlier, the gunpowder works consisted of many water mills where the ingredients were ground together, then processed. Originally large, broad waterwheels were used, but in the late nineteenth century locally manufactured turbines were installed within the older masonry wheelpits. Gilkes of Kendal, famous turbine manufacturers for over a hundred years, is a legacy of the once thriving powered industries, which were concentrated in the River Kent catchment area. The remains of Gilkes turbines can be found at mines, quarries, bobbin mills, saw mills, gunpowder works and other sites.

In common with all rural areas, the Lake District had its scatter of corn mills, many with medieval origins. Although these mills were essential to the daily life, they were operated as small-scale rural trades rather than as 'industrial' sites. Nevertheless, within some villages, especially at the focal point for old trade routes, the old mill buildings may still survive as an attractive reminder of the former dependence on water power.

Extensive sheep farming in medieval times led to the establishment of an important woollen industry centred on Kendal, with the Kent, Sprint and Mint Rivers converging on this important market town. By the mid-fourteenth century the Lake District had almost 150 fulling mills where water-driven wooden stocks pounded hand-woven material with soft brown soaps to mat or felt the cloth. Before water power was used, men walked on the cloth in troughs, to felt it, hence the common name 'Walk Mill' for early woollen mills. Grasmere and Ambleside had a cluster of medieval fulling mills and names such as Stock Lane and Stock Bridge no doubt refer to this industry. At Hawkshead, Tenter Hill is a reference to the hillside where cloth was stretched on the tenterhooks, to dry in the sun.

During the second half of the eighteenth century the effects of the

Plate 29 This attractive view towards Coniston is essentially a landscape of industry. Almost hidden, there is evidence of copper mining, slate quarrying, mills for textiles and bobbins, an iron forge, a tannery, quays for water transport and a once busy railway terminus *(Andrew Lowe)*

industrial revolution spread through northern England. In the Lake District it was a revolution in the scale of production rather than a power revolution – steam engines were not introduced into the local woollen industry until the 1850s. The fulling mills, together with the domestic system, were superseded by the factory system for both spinning and weaving woollens. Other textile mills for spinning cotton and flax were introduced after the 1770s, often on the sites of redundant fulling mills. Such large mills required the dependable supply of water from the larger rivers to turn broad, powerful waterwheels connected to a network of line shafting for the spinning and weaving machinery. Characteristically, the wool carding or weaving mills were usually three storeys high, but the cotton spinning mills reached four or five storeys in typical Lancashire style with the regular rows of small paned windows. These were the tallest buildings in the Lake District, so dominant not just in physical terms, but also in relation to the local economic and social life.

Wool was a local raw material from the fell areas and consequently the woollen mills were widely scattered within the rural areas, for example at Caldbeck, Keswick, Coniston and Staveley as well as in the growing towns of Kendal, Ulverston and Cockermouth. Cotton, on the other hand, was imported from America into Lancaster and Whitehaven, so that Lancashire cotton spinning companies established mills in these two towns and also on good water power sites at Ulverston, Spark Bridge, Backbarrow and Staveley (see Fig 19). At Barley Bridge, Staveley there survives a fine example of a late eighteenth century stone-built cotton mill, which later became a prosperous woollen mill, and then a bobbin mill and today is a paper packaging factory. In the lowland rural areas locally grown flax was spun and woven into linen during the mid eighteenth century in mills at Cockermouth, Cleator, Egremont, Whitehaven, Ulverston and in the Milnthorpe area. These mills were well located to supply great quantities of sailcloth and sheeting, so essential for the coastal shipping – the vital economic lifeline before the coming of the railways.

Although most of the towns had textile factories with many still recognisable today, it is in the rural areas that the old mills and their workers communities provide the clues to understanding this working

(opposite) Buttermere and the high volcanic central fells (Simon Crouch). (over page) The Langdale Pikes. On the slopes of Pike of Stickle, the peak on the left of the photograph, prehistoric man roughed out stone axes from the fine-grained volcanic ash which makes up this impressive mountain range (Norman Duerden)

landscape. Many operatives were needed at the mills, so the mill terraced houses, together with the mill manager's house and possibly a workhouse, are distinct features to look for. Staveley's Barley Bridge mill, with its clock and bell tower, has nearby rows of terraced houses, Mealbank near Kendal has various mills and houses, Penny Bridge flax mill has its dozen workers houses, and Millbeck near Keswick was originally a woollen community attractively sited on the lower slopes of Skiddaw.

Waste products from the cotton, woollen and flax mills encouraged the development of paper mills in the late seventeenth century, where good water supplies powered machinery for pulping the rags. To the north of Ambleside the name Papermill Coppice dates back to the 1680s. Much larger-scale paper mills developed after the mid-eighteenth century especially near Kendal. Cowan Head mill is now closed, but it is still a prominent feature indicating what most rurally based industry would have looked like, in contrast to the urban concentrations. Nearby, the village of Burneside is dominated visually, economically and socially by James Cropper's paper mills.

We have seen in this chapter that the industrial landscapes are not merely a collection of relics, ruins and waste heaps, but are features of a living landscape. Not all the various industries were in operation at any one time, but the main period of prosperity for most rural crafts and industries was between 1750 and 1850. Through ingenuity, adaptation and careful management of resources some aspects of the Lake District industrial life have survived into the twentieth century. It is therefore important that when admiring the view we must not be over-awed by the sheer scale of the fells, lakes and valleys and forget about the smaller industrial elements (Plate 29). Scattered over the fells, clustered in the small towns and villages of the valleys, and hidden amongst the woods are significant features of our heritage. Fortunately, selected sites have been preserved and made available for the public to appreciate and enjoy, so that future generations can come to the Lake District and understand that this area was once a very important landscape of industry.

(opposite above) Upper Eskdale was acquired by the monks of Furness Abbey in 1242 and converted into a huge sheep pasture. From the fell on the right of the photograph, the Roman fort of Hardknott perches eyrie-like above the dale (Bill Rollinson).
(opposite) Blea Tarn, the dark blue tarn, was appropriately named in the language of the Irish-Norse settlers who colonised the fells in the ninth and tenth centuries (Simon Crouch)

6
ROADS, CANALS
AND RAILWAYS

SURPRISINGLY little has been written about the effects of roads, canals and railways on landscapes despite the fact that communications are a vital component of landscape development. The prolific railway literature tends to concentrate on minute detail of the lines, engines, stations and rolling stock, but it usually says little about precisely why the lines were needed, and next to nothing about the effects which the lines had on the areas which they served; the canal literature is not dissimilar. But roads, and their effects on the landscape, have been almost totally ignored, despite (and probably because of) their commonplace nature.

The various means of transport employed in and around the Lake District over the last 2,000 years have been a fundamental part of the overall economic, social and political development of the area, and therefore of its landscape as well. For example the Roman roads were part of a military defensive system serving numerous forts; the continuing importance of these roads is reflected in how many of them are still in use today. More recently the turnpikes, canals and railways were built to allow easier movement of agricultural and industrial products to and between the rapidly growing towns, and the improved accessibility drastically altered both town and country. Transport routes themselves barely altered the landscape but because they were an integral part of the economic changes, many other features of the landscape were often significantly changed as a result of improvements in communications. Thus, without building their roads the Romans would not have been able to defend this north-western corner of their empire, the medieval towns would not have been able to trade and grow, from Elizabethan times wool would not have been able to reach and to be traded from the market at Kendal, and the first tourists would never have got anywhere near the Lakes. Without the canals the movement of heavy goods to and from Kendal in particular would not have been possible, and the consequent early development of towns, industry and mining would have been much delayed. And finally the railways, also built to carry coal and iron, were eventually important in opening up the Lakes to many more tourists, bringing them quickly and cheaply to Windermere, Coniston and Keswick.

But the Lake District does not easily lend itself to the building of lines of communication. The level of economic (and sometimes political) demand for transport determines whether or not lines of communication are built, but the landscape then imposes constraints on their routes. And in mountainous terrain the choice of routes is especially difficult for canals and railways. In the Lake District the net result is that roads have always provided the backbone of communications; the canals are peripheral (none lying within the National Park), and the railways, although of great importance for a hundred years or so, barely penetrated into the area, and are now reduced to little more than a ring of lines around the Lakes.

ROADS

Roman roads

The first roads of which we have any clear knowledge were constructed by the Roman armies in the years after the invasion of northern England in AD78–79 (see Chapter 2). The Romans were intent on conquering the whole of Britain, but eventually had to settle for defending a northern border which ran from the Solway to the mouth of the Tyne (along the Stanegate, and subsequently Hadrian's Wall). The frontier was continued down the coast to Moresby (near Whitehaven) as a line of forts linked and backed up by roads. The Romans were evidently little interested in the Lake District itself, as only three or four roads went through the fells (Fig 20).

Their main road south led from Carlisle to Brougham, and then on through the Lune Gorge. This route runs along the very eastern edge of the Lakeland fells and its principal fascination is that so many later routes have followed in its footsteps – though none has followed it precisely. From Brougham its course cannot now be seen for the first three miles (5 km), but it can then be followed as 'The Street' for over five miles (8 km) towards Crosby Ravensworth. It turns to pass through the British settlement at Ewe Close (see Plate 12), and climbs over Coalpit Hill before making a steady descent towards Tebay and the fort at Low Borrow Bridge in the Lune Gorge. From here there was a branch to Watercrook (Kendal), whilst the main road continued southwards on the east bank of the River Lune.

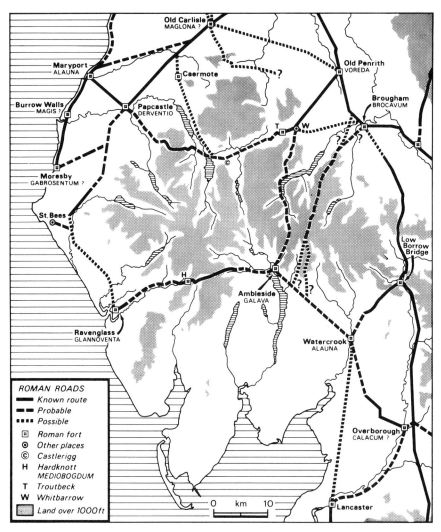

Fig 20 Roman roads

Of the Roman roads through the Lake District the most important was probably the route from Watercrook to Ravenglass, for it appears in the *Antonine Itinerary*, a list of the main post roads of the Empire compiled in Rome in the second or third century. The central section of this route over Wrynose and Hardknott Passes is well known, and easy to follow, but the precise course of most of the rest of the route has yet to be fixed. Starting from Watercrook it is not even certain where the road crossed the River Kent; it probably went via Staveley, and beyond here the best line yet found is parallel to the minor road running from Hill Farm, through Broadgate to Allen Knott. The central section over the passes was described by Ian Richmond in 1949 and anyone wishing to follow it should consult his classic paper. But at the western end of Hardknott Pass the road once again disappears into farmland, still over 8 miles (12.9km) from the port of Ravenglass. There are no Roman roads in Cumbria south of this route, which indicates how un-important, strategically or economically, southern Lakeland was to the Romans.

The most famous Roman road in the Lakes is undoubtedly High Street, but its course is little known in precise detail, even in the central section where it is supposed to run at over 2000ft (610m) for 8 miles (12.9km). In truth there are only two or three obvious sections (for example between High Street summit and the Straits of Riggindale) and the whole route requires a new survey. In particular, its routes both south of the summit and north of Elder Beck are not known. It would certainly not have been an easy route, much of it above the tree line, and the Romans probably used it, but whether they actually *built* a road along the whole of this line is, at best, unproven. The recent detailed description of a parallel Roman road over Kirkstone Pass, only a short distance to the west, is a much more likely route for them to have chosen, involving only half the ascent, and having frequent water supplies for their animals (something which High Street lacks).

This latter road from Ambleside over Kirkstone ended near Whit-barrow, where it joined the second east–west road through the hills. This road ran from Old Penrith to Troutbeck, and then probably con-tinued via Keswick and the Whinlatter Pass to Papcastle (Cockermouth); here it joined the network of roads along the Solway coast. The road direct to the coast at Maryport is still followed by footpaths and roads for over half its length, whilst the main road from Papcastle north-west to Carlisle is now largely overlain by the A595.

Medieval and packhorse roads
After the departure of the Romans, no new roads were to be built in the Lake District for almost 1500 years and yet, during this long period, it is certain that most of the roads in the area came into being. These were not the engineered and metalled roads of the Romans, but roads which made and maintained themselves by the continual passage of man and beast. For the Dark Ages there is virtually no historical record of roads, but it is clear that as the whole area became more densely settled, tracks would have been created piecemeal from one farm to the next, and then from one village to the next, simply in order to enable the in-habitants to trade and barter. Thus by the end of the medieval period most of what are now the minor roads of the Lake District had come into being.

In the twelfth century the monasteries were established, and their

133

records show some of the roads they used to reach their far-flung estates; other evidence from this period includes various charters, grants, and deeds which mention roads as boundaries to plots of land. However, the thirteenth century saw the first real urban growth, based on an upsurge of trade; the bulk of the goods had to be carried from town to town by road, there being few navigable rivers in the area. Apart from Keswick, these towns lay around the edge of the Lake District, the most important being Kendal, Ulverston, Egremont, Cockermouth and Penrith. The one solid piece of historical evidence for the main roads at this time is the Gough Map, often dated at c1360, but probably originally compiled eighty years earlier. It shows a road from Carlisle south to Penrith, Shap, Kendal and Lancaster with various routes off to the east, but no roads entering the central Lake District. Equally, the various monarchs, whose travels are increasingly well recorded, saw no reason to visit this mountainous area.

In fact the roads in the Lake District remained narrow and unimproved until the mid-eighteenth century; the best impression of what they were like can be gained from looking at the condition of tracks in the mountains today. The passes through the hills must have been used from a very early date in order to avoid very long journeys around the

Plate 30 The start of Styhead Pass leading from Wasdale Head chapel beneath the slopes of Great Gable of Borrowdale *(Paul Hindle)*

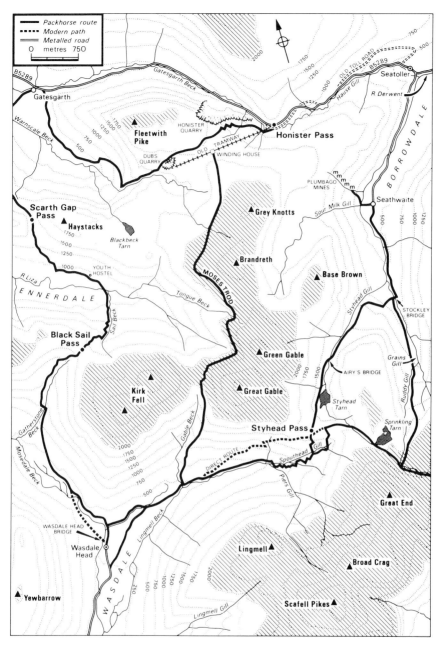

Fig 21 Mountain passes

hills, and most of them have engineered zig-zags to ease the gradient for their use by packhorses. No one knows when these zig-zags were made – a likely date is the sixteenth and seventeenth centuries – but this probably represents the only serious road construction between the departure of the Romans and the mid-eighteenth-century turnpikes. Typically, the tracks are only a few feet wide, and often have quite sharp corners; there are many good examples, including the southern side of Styhead Pass (the old route) (Plate 30), the Rossett Gill pony track, the Langdale side of Stake Pass (recently repaired) and the northern side of Gatescarth Pass (Fig 21). These last two passes were described by Thomas West in his *Guide to the Lakes* first published in 1778; Gatescarth is described as 'winding, steep and narrow', whilst Stake Pass has a longer description: 'Whoever chooses an Alpine journey, of a very extraordinary nature may return .... over the *Stake* .... The ride is the wildest that can be imagined .... The road makes many traverses so close, that at every flexure it seems almost to return into itself, and such as are advancing in different traverses, appear to go different ways.'

A peculiar group of tracks were those leading from remote outlying settlements to a church where the dead had to be buried; where these routes were seldom used for any other purpose they became known as *corpse roads*. There were many such roads, though corpses have not been carried along them for several hundred years. Two routes were well enough known to have appeared on recent Ordnance Survey maps; the first from Wasdale Head across Burnmoor to the nearest parish church at Boot in Eskdale, and the second, from the village of Mardale Green (now submerged beneath Haweswater) via Swindale to Shap.

Corpse roads and the mountain passes are in fact both special types of packhorse track which constituted the road system of the Lake

Plate 31 Packhorse bridge, Wasdale Head *(W. Rollinson)*

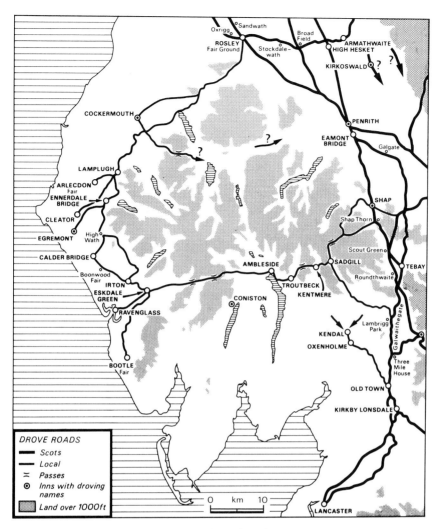

Fig 22 Drove roads in the Lake District

District from medieval times until the turnpikes were built. Kendal was the main centre of trade (especially for wool); and from here groups of packhorses worked across the Lakeland hills to Whitehaven, Cockermouth, Ulverston, Hawkshead, Cartmel, Orton, and Penrith, as well as to the rest of England. In the lowlands these tracks have, for the most part, been overlain by modern roads, with their original zig-zags and steep gradients eased and improved. A few still survive – such as the route along the southern shore of Ullswater from Patterdale to Howtown. Packhorse bridges have received rather more attention than the tracks, no doubt because they are picturesque landscape features. There are over seventy of these bridges, some well known, but many are hidden in obscure places, on tracks now little used. They sometimes cross surprisingly small streams, but packhorses often carried valuable goods and it was too risky to drive the horses through the water. The bridges are usually narrow, and with low parapets or none at all. The only one to be dated is that at Calva Hall (near Dean, 1697) but the general consensus is that many were built between 1660 and 1760, a period of great growth of trade throughout the district.

Drove roads

An important component of the local economy was the rearing of cattle, which were then driven to the ever growing towns further south. There were two quite distinct aspects of this trade; Scots cattle being driven through or around the Lake District, with local cattle joining them en route (Fig 22). From Scotland cattle came across the Solway or through Carlisle, and converged on Penrith before moving on into Lancashire or Yorkshire. Just north of the Lake District there was an important cattle fair at Rosley, where local cattle from the Solway coast joined those from Scotland. There were also spring fairs at various places along the coast (such as Arlecdon, Boonwood and Bootle) for cattle which had been kept over winter. Some cattle were driven across Hardknott and Wrynose passes to Ambleside and Troutbeck, then over the Garburn Pass into Kentmere and finally across to Longsleddale before turning to join the main droving routes. The main drove road to the south led from Penrith to Shap and then into the Lune Gorge. Once past Low Borrow Bridge it climbed up the west side of the valley along a section described as early as the late twelfth century as *Galwaithegate* (ie the Galloway Road) and known later as Scotch Lane. The trade clearly has a long history which continued until it was abruptly curtailed by the construction of the railways (Fig 22).

Originally the drove roads were wide open tracks running from one overnight pasture to the next. As much of the area was not enclosed until the years around 1800 (see below), these roads simply traversed open land, and where they did pass through farm land, became wide winding lanes between walls, following the lie of the land. Today such roads can still be seen, though most are now enclosed; they usually still have wide grass verges with a recent narrow strip of metalling down the middle.

Sands routes

The two southern peninsulas of Cartmel and Furness had always been difficult of access; the usual way to reach them was to travel across the sands at low tide. The route is known to have been in use in the Middle Ages, and continued to flourish until the coastal railway was com-

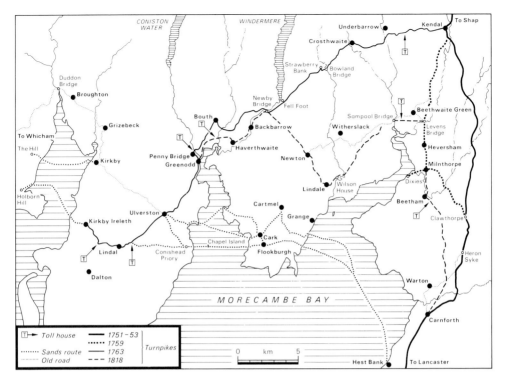

Fig 23 Routes across the sands

pleted in 1857; indeed, for eighty years before that date, a daily public coach ran across the sands. The reason for the use of this route was simple – from Ulverston to Lancaster on the hilly packhorse route via Kendal (later turnpiked in 1763) was 41 miles (66 km); across the sands it was a mere 19 (30 km) (Fig 23). The sands were so commonly used that West's *Guide* (1778) began its tour of the Lakes by that route, noting that it was 'a journey of little more danger than any other', and adding that 'On a fine day there is not a more pleasant seaside journey in the Kingdom.'

The route left the 'mainland' at Hest Bank, and after some eight miles (13km) came ashore between Kent's Bank and Grange, the precise route changing with the shifting channels of the Rivers Keer and Kent. The route next traversed the Cartmel peninsula via Flookburgh (then a place of some importance due to the sands traffic) and crossed the Levens sands (passing Chapel Island) for Ulverston. Travellers wishing to continue around the Cumbrian coast would then cross Low Furness, and take to the sands again at Ireleth, this time crossing the Duddon estuary. Before the mid-eighteenth-century road improvements, anyone travelling from Lancaster to Whitehaven would probably go via this route instead of going through the hills. But not everyone enjoyed it; John Wesley writing in 1759 said that he would 'advise no stranger to go this way. He may go round by Kendal and Keswick, often in less time, always with less expense, and far less trial of his patience.'

Turnpikes

The ever increasing amount of trade and the consequent road traffic put such a strain on roads (most of which had never been surfaced or engineered) that some new form of maintenance and improvement was needed. Individual parishes had generally done little to maintain the roads which passed through them, and the solution lay in the creation of turnpikes. Local merchants, landowners and others would put forward a bill to Parliament to allow them to improve a certain road, and to charge tolls for those who then used it. Typically a turnpike act began with a preamble such as 'Whereas the road [from A to B] is very much out of repair, narrow and incommodious for travellers, and some parts thereof are in so ruinous a condition as to be unsafe for the passage of cattle and carriages, and the said road cannot be sufficiently amended, widened, altered and kept in repair, by the ordinary course of law. . . .' Thus, in their early days turnpike trusts simply took over existing roads and carried out necessary works on the worst sections.

The first turnpikes in this area were four roads converging on Whitehaven, created by the town's Harbour Act of 1739; they were followed by an abortive act of 1750 to continue one of these roads from Egremont down the coast to the Duddon estuary (Fig 24). 1753 saw six more turnpike acts in Cumbria, including roads from Penrith to Chalk Beck (now the B5305), Workington to Cockermouth (though the act's continuation to Carlisle via Wigton was never implemented) and the road over Shap (from the Lancashire county boundary at Heron Syke right through to Carlisle). There were military as well as economic reasons for the building of the Shap turnpike; Bonnie Prince Charlie had travelled that way in 1745, and both his army and the English following his retreat had great difficulty in negotiating the old road.

Another important turnpike act for this area was passed in 1762, improving roads through the central fells – though their description in the act takes a tortuous course: from Hesket Newmarket to Cockermouth, Keswick, Kendal and Windermere, with a branch from Keswick to Penrith (ie great lengths of what are now the A66 and A591). Finally, the old packhorse track from Kendal to Ulverston and Kirkby Ireleth was turnpiked in 1763, and a direct route from Carlisle to Keswick via Skillbeck (1767) brought to an end the brief 'turnpike

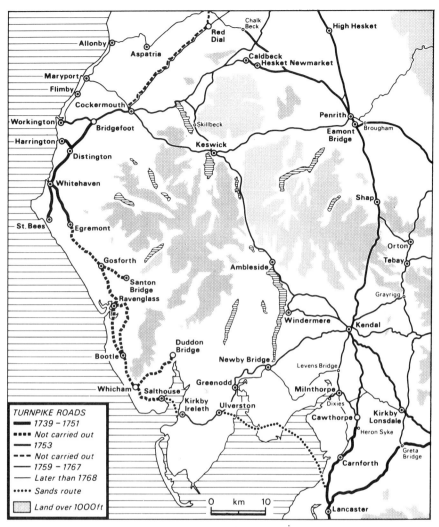

Fig 24 Turnpikes in the Lake District

mania' in the Lake District. There were no more acts in Cumbria until 1794, and the only later one of any importance was the Levens Bridge to Greenodd Act of 1818 (now the A590).

Thus within a few years in the middle of the eighteenth century a mechanism was put in place for the maintenance of the main roads into the Lake District. It is no great surprise to see the beginnings of tourism at this time; the descriptions by Gray, Hutchinson and West were all made between 1769 and 1778, and Arthur Young's *Tour* had been published in 1770. Young was interested in agriculture (which was then beginning to improve rapidly) and he also gives a few terse comments about the roads; of the Kendal to Windermere road he says; 'Turnpike; now making. What is finished is as good, firm, level a road

141

Plate 32 Huck's Bridge on the new Shap turnpike built around 1830. The old road crossed the river at High Borrow Bridge 250m beyond the new bridge *(Paul Hindle)*

as any in the world. I nowhere remember a better', though others were 'vilely cut up' or simply 'very bad'. Cumbria's population doubled during the eighteenth century, and the improvements in roads were but one part of the whole process of economic and social change which was going on. By 1801 Kendal's population was almost 7,000; carriers' wagons had taken over from the packhorses, and stage coaches were a common sight in the town.

Some turnpikes were substantially improved in the 1820s when they were re-aligned, and had completely new sections built, usually in order to ease the gradients. Substantial lengths of the Shap route were rebuilt according to plans by Mr. McAdam, indeed most of the route from Strawberry Bank (3 miles [5km] south of Kendal) to Shap village was laid out on a completely new line (Plate 32). But this was exceptional, elsewhere there was much tinkering with short lengths. A typical example of the small-scale improvements was the building of the road alongside Grasmere in 1823, replacing the route past Dove Cottage and over White Moss; the new road was longer but virtually level. Further north the same road had to be rebuilt when the level of Thirlmere was raised in the early 1890s. The original line of this road south of Keswick led straight out of the town square, and up a steep hill (West described it as 'somewhat quick'), whilst the turnpike to Penrith left the town independently, going along the narrow lane past Castlerigg stone circle. Both these roads are clearly shown on Donald's map of 1774 (Fig 25).

Fig 25 Donald's Cumberland, 1774, Keswick area

Getting across to Cartmel and Furness continued to be a problem, barely helped by the 1763 turnpike from Kendal (see Fig 23). A track ran across the peat mosses from Beethwaite Green (Levens) but it seems to have been little used, the Sands route being preferred. Even the creation of the more southerly turnpike from Levens to Newby Bridge and Greenodd in 1818 did little to reduce the traffic across the sands, which continued unabated until the coastal railway line was opened in 1857. Thus the turnpikes, most established in the 1750s and 1760s, then improved and added to in the period 1815–35, had a dramatic impact on communications within and beyond the Lake District. Goods could be carried in greater quantity and much more rapidly than before, but the days of the turnpikes were numbered. Largely due to railway competition they were dissolved between 1870 and 1885, the county authorities taking over responsibility for roads and bridges.

143

Enclosure roads

One further major alteration to the road system occurred, principally in the early years of the nineteenth century, caused by the Parliamentary enclosure of large areas of common land and waste. One major reason for this was the greatly increased demand for agricultural produce during the Napoleonic Wars. Great tracts around the edge of the Lake District which had been open grazing land were redesigned into a new enclosed landscape by surveyors who, more often than not, imposed straight lines and right angles on the landscape. Their plans usually survive, though we can only rarely glimpse what the landscape was like before their changes. Enclosure roads were commonly laid out at a standard width of 40 or 50ft (12 or 15m), representing a hangover over the medieval custom that a traveller had to be allowed to get around any foundrous section of road. Most of these roads were not surfaced when they were created, though sometimes the Enclosure Acts stipulated precise details; in the Cartmel enclosure one particular road was to 'be covered ten feet [3m] wide with broken stones not bigger than a goose's egg . . . . nine inches [22cm] in thickness on the crown of the road'. The best examples of enclosure roads and landscapes are to be seen around the northern fringes of the Lakes, especially in the area of the old Inglewood Forest, north-west of Penrith (Plate 33). J. C. Curwen, writing in 1815 noted that 'A line of commons but a few years since reached from Workington to Carlisle, ... out of thirty five miles [56km], twenty five [40km] at least might have been passed over commons, the whole of which is now enclosed.'

Plate 33 The A6 now overlies the Roman road between Penrith and Carlisle. The fort of Old Penrith was situated in the field immediately behind the large farm at the centre of the photograph *(Paul Hindle)*

Enclosure not only allowed increased agricultural production, it also improved access between the farmer and his market, to the mutual benefit of all concerned. Enclosure brought about as drastic a change to some parts of the local road system as the turnpikes had previously done to the main roads.

Recent changes

By the early nineteenth century the road network of the Lake District was much as we know it today. Throughout the nineteenth and twentieth centuries both commercial and tourist traffic on the roads increased steadily. Many tourists arrived in the area on the new railways, but from thereon the roads remained virtually the only way to get about. On the roads, carts gave way to wagons and lorries, and carriages to buses; individual transport was also improved, first by the bicycle from the mid-1880s, and then by the private car during the twentieth century. Unfortunately, much of this growth coincided with the demise of the turnpikes in the 1870s and 1880s, and many roads deteriorated. Matters were so bad in some places that the English Lake District Association was set up in 1876, partly to maintain and improve roads; they even tried to improve Hardknott Pass in the 1880s, but the scheme was not a success.

In the last 150 years, few completely new roads have been built; instead, existing roads have been surfaced, widened, straightened, made into dual carriageways, or had their gradients eased. The only large-scale exceptions to this have been the M6, and much of the A66. The M6, completed in 1970, carves its way through the Lune Gorge, taking a very similar route to the Roman road, several drove roads and turnpikes, and the railway. Only the A6 over Shap takes a different route, but all these routes are close to each other between Shap village and Penrith. The A66 was recently the subject of much debate, many people suggesting that the much needed improvements should take the road around the National Park (north of Skiddaw) rather than along its original route through it. Despite strong opposition, the latter option was chosen, and there are now substantial new sections between Penrith, Keswick and Cockermouth.

Roads, which have been a fundamental part of the economic and social growth of the Lakes since Roman times, are once again, within the area, virtually the only means of transport available. It is now the road network which provides access, whether for local residents to travel to school, work, recreation or the shops, for tourists to walk, climb, gaze or throng, or for drivers of heavy goods vehicles to transport goods in and out of the area. Unfortunately, roads are often seen only as scars on the landscape. But there is no shortage of features which can be reviewed in that way – car parks, housing estates, camping and caravanning sites, quarries, regimented coniferous forests, and reservoirs with 'draw-down' shorelines, to name but a few. Beside some of these, roads are a minor intrusion, and they clearly encourage trade and tourism. But the people they bring in are themselves a problem; if there are too many visitors to the Lakes, then sheer numbers will obscure, alter or destroy the very landscape features which so many tourists have come to see. This dilemma presents numerous problems to those who are currently responsible for planning access to the Lake District. In planning terms, at least, roads are now seen as important; yet they have always been a vital and historic part of the landscape, and deserve more study than they have yet received.

CANALS

Although the roads were being improved in the second half of the eighteenth century, it was still difficult to move heavy or bulky goods; the solution for places near navigable water was to use boats, and this is a major reason for the growth of towns around the Cumbrian coast (notably Whitehaven, Workington and Maryport). The rivers of the Lake District are little suited to navigation; the Derwent was once navigable to Cockermouth, the Esk perhaps to Eskdale Green, and the Leven to Backbarrow. Some goods could be sent by lake; in Elizabethan times copper was transported across Derwentwater to the smelter at Brigham, above Keswick (see Chapter 5). Later both Windermere and Coniston Water were extensively used for moving charcoal; the furnace at Backbarrow, established in 1711, was a frequent destination for cargoes of charcoal, shipped down either lake, and then by road to the furnace, where iron ore arrived by boat from Low Furness (Chapter 5). Copper and slate were also shipped down Coniston Water, and then on by cart to Penny Bridge or Greenodd for trans-shipment. Around Morecambe Bay it was common to sail boats a short distance up the rivers, or simply beach them on the sands and unload them at low tide. In this way various places become ports – including Ulverston, Greenodd, and Milnthorpe (the port for Kendal).

Ulverston Canal
The town of Ulverston lay over a mile from the sea, and in 1791 there was a proposal to build a ship canal. The 'canal mania' of the 1790s was just beginning, local exports of iron ore and slate were growing rapidly, and the proposers saw the hamlet of Barrow as a potential

rival. An Act was obtained in 1793, and the canal opened late in 1796; it was described as the shortest, deepest and widest canal in England, it was only 1³/₈ miles (2km) in length, terminated in a large basin near the town, and had a single lock into the Leven estuary. In order to encourage slate traffic, the canal company built a road from Kirkby to Netherhouses in 1798, and this route was evidently preferred, despite being twice as long as the previous route which involved taking slate down to ships beached in the Duddon estuary. The main problem facing the Ulverston Canal was the erratic behaviour of the channel of the River Leven, which sometimes shifted towards the Cartmel side of the estuary, making entry into the canal difficult. Nevertheless, for a time, the canal prospered, trading mainly in agricultural products, coal, slate, iron and timber, as well as in copper and 'spiritous liquors'; it reached a peak of 944 vessels in 1846. But then decline set in rapidly, largely due to the development of the Furness Railway serving the new ports of Barrow and Piel. The death knell was sounded when the railway around the bay was completed in 1857, and the railway bought the canal in 1862; it was last used in 1916 and finally abandoned in 1945.

There was probably another short canal at Lindale, built by John Wilkinson, the iron master, to transport peat to his furnace, but no traces now remain.

Lancaster Canal

The most important canal venture to serve the Lake District was the Lancaster Canal, which, even though it did not go beyond Kendal, provided an outlet for the produce of a large part of the Lakes. The canal was originally promoted by Lancaster merchants who wanted to improve communications, in particular to bring limestone from the north and coal from the south. The first plan was drawn up in 1772 but nothing was done; by 1791 an anonymous writer said that it was 'no longer a Question of Choice but Necessity. . . . a Canal is now become as necessary an Appendage to a Manufacturing or Commercial Town as a Turnpike Road.' Things then moved rapidly, with the first Act obtained in 1792 and a second to provide a link to the sea at Glasson in 1793 (not built until 1825).

Much of the canal's early history is concerned with its southern section, south of Preston, where there was prolonged dispute with other canal companies. The northern section from Preston as far as Tewitfield was completed by the end of 1797, but the completion of the final 14¹/₂ miles (23km) to Kendal was continually deferred for over twenty years. Finally a new Act was obtained in 1807 altering the original

147

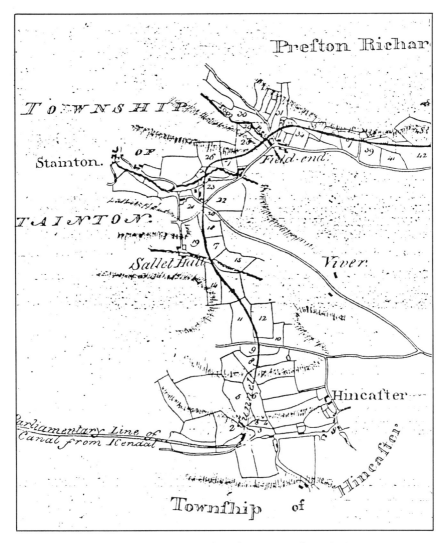

Fig 26 Lancaster Canal: Parliamentary plan, 1806

route; work began in 1813 and was completed in 1819, including the flight of 8 locks at Tewitfield, and the 377 yard (340m) tunnel at Hincaster (Fig 26).

The town of Kendal was so keen to have good canal facilities that it built the terminal basin, wharves and warehouses at its own expense. The canal sold land to the Kendal Gas Company in 1824, which brought in its regular coal supplies by canal. Kendal's outport at Milnthorpe declined, and instead, goods to and from distant places were trans-shipped at Hest Bank where the canal looped very close to the coast; this continued until 1831. Trade on the canal included all types of cargo – grain, timber, coal, chemicals for the gunpowder

Plate 34 The Lancaster Canal passing the limestone crags of Hutton Roof near Farleton *(Paul Hindle)*

mills, and even Welsh slate were carried into Kendal, and return cargoes included limestone, slate and wool. From 1820 there were packet services from Kendal in competition with stage coaches, which, even though improved in 1833, still took 6½ hours for the run to Lancaster (Plate 34).

The basic problem with the Lancaster Canal was that it was never connected to the rest of the canal system. In 1803 the company had built a 'temporary' tramroad between Preston and the detached southern section of the canal, but this meant that goods had to be transshipped twice. The canal's traffic was progressively reduced as railways were built alongside, the final section being the completion of the railway north from Lancaster as far as Kendal in 1846. But from 1850 to 1858 there was a traffic-sharing agreement between the canal and the railway, the former still carrying coal and heavy goods to Kendal, even though for carriage to Windermere these goods had to be carted through Kendal from the canal basin to the station. The northern section of the canal was finally leased to the London and North Western Railway in 1864, and bought outright by them in 1886. Traffic declined steadily through the years of railway competition, though it is interesting to note that as late as 1894 the cheapest route for the import of cement for the construction of the Thirlmere waterworks was through Glasson docks and along the canal. Traffic between Lancaster and Kendal ceased in 1944, and the northern most 6 miles (10km)

149

were drained in 1955. The M6 now cuts the canal in three places, first at the top of Tewitfield locks, although the remaining section to Hincaster is still largely in water, as it is still used as a feeder and for research. It is possible to walk along most of the canal, apart from where it has been cut by the A591 just north of Hincaster; restoration of the canal would not be totally impossible.

Clearly the impact of the canal age on the Lake District was limited, principally by the nature of the terrain, as well as by the limited profits which might have been made from building canals in such a poor and remote area. However, the canals which were built did allow the increased export of some of the heavier goods such as slate, iron and limestone, whilst certain imports had their effect too; the arrival of bricks and Welsh slate, for example, eventually altered local architectural styles. The import of much cheaper coal was undoubtedly a great boon to both householders and manufacturers. Kendal's population grew by a third between 1811 and 1831, and the whole area served by Kendal (and for that matter by Ulverston) benefitted from improved access which the canals gave them to the rest of the country.

RAILWAYS

To attempt a complete and detailed history of Lakeland railways here would be impossible; in any case railway history is hardly a neglected topic, and therefore only the bare bones of railway development will be sketched (Fig 27). The strangest fact about most railways in the Lake District is how short a period they endured; their development began in the 1840s, but within 130 years little more than a single line around the Lakes survived. And yet within that short period the impact they had on the area was immense. Most of the lines were built for industrial traffic and the sheer scale of the growth of the mining and industrial areas, and of towns such as Workington and Millom, was unprecedented. The railways were fundamental to the mid-nineteenth-century industrial growth of western Cumbria. Moreover the lines helped tourism to take off until the private car took over as the commonest means of transport.

In the eighteenth century there were a number of waggonways and tramways notably around the already important town and port of Whitehaven, but these were not in any real sense precursors of the railways. Railways were late to reach even the fringes of the Lake District. The first was a short line from Maryport to Arkleby pit (near Aspatria) in 1840; it was eventually continued through to Carlisle by 1845 (which was already linked to Newcastle). Seeing this development as a

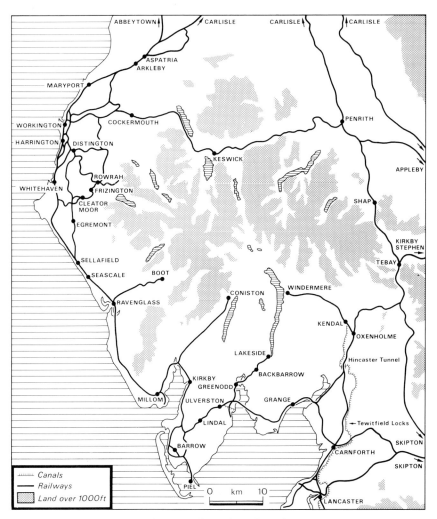

Fig 27 Railways and canals in the Lake District

potential threat, Lord Lowther had the line extended from Maryport to Whitehaven by 1847.

Further south, the Furness Railway had been opened in 1846 in order to transport the rich haematite iron ores from Lindal, and slate from Kirkby, to the sea principally through the port of Barrow (then only a tiny village) and also via Roa Island (Piel), both routes ignoring Ulverston and its canal. At the same time plans were afoot to link Whitehaven and Furness by rail; this was not planned as a west coast main line, but simply to allow the railway companies to reach more mineral deposits. By 1850 this link was complete, and it was possible for traffic to run from Furness via Whitehaven and Maryport to Carlisle. Such a journey involved five different railway companies, and

151

was notoriously slow (*plus ça change!*). Whitehaven tunnel was not opened until 1852; until then through traffic had to use a mineral line through the town. The technically difficult and expensive southern link around the sands to Carnforth was not completed until 1857, but it ended the traffic across the sands overnight, and made the Ulverston Canal redundant. This line, cutting across the Leven and Kent estuaries with long embankments and bridges, allowed the reclamation of substantial areas of what had formerly been salt marsh.

All these locally inspired and inward-looking lines were very different to the various grand designs for a west coast main line. In 1840, after much investigation, two Parliamentary commissioners recommended that the main line from Lancaster should go northwards over Shap, ignoring the various schemes which had been put forward for a coastal route. We can only guess at how differently the west Cumbrian coast and the western Lake District might have developed if such a route had been adopted. But the Shap route was opened in 1846, causing, amongst other things, the rapid demise of cattle droving over Shap, and the sudden growth of Tebay as a railway settlement. It was immediately followed by the opening of the first line into the Lake District, from Kendal to the hamlet of Birthwaite (now Windermere) in 1847. It had originally been planned to end this line just short of Ambleside, and perhaps later extend it over Dunmail Raise. But Wordsworth (and others) had objected violently even though he was hardly in a position to object to outsiders coming to see the area, having written so much about the Lakes, and thus having himself attracted more and more visitors. The scheme resurfaced in 1875 and 1886, this time opposed by Ruskin and Rawnsley whilst proposals for lines in Borrowdale and Ennerdale in the 1880s also came to nought.

There were numerous other lines which were proposed but which never came to fruition; for example, as early as 1845 there were two schemes to link the Furness Railway with the new main line, one direct from Milnthorpe and another from Windermere, each leading to Newby Bridge, and thence via Backbarrow and Greenodd to Ulverston (Fig 28).

The Windermere line was promoted largely by Kendal, first to give the town a link to the main line, and second to encourage the tourist trade. New industries such as shoe making were replacing the declining wool trade, and there was an expanding paper mill at Burneside which imported both coal and raw materials by rail. From 1849 Kendal had a fortnightly cattle market and the cattle were then taken south by train. At Windermere, the station was far from the lake, its line pointing towards Ambleside in the forlorn hope of being extended. An hotel was built, and coaches took tourists and day-trippers down to the lake or on into Lakeland. In 1801 Dorothy Wordsworth would note in her diary when a chaise passed Dove Cottage, but with the road improvements and the railways feeding tourists into the area, over 40 carriages a day travelled over Dunmail Raise by 1855. Windermere became a fashionable place for Manchester merchants to have their second homes; some even commuted, whilst others retired there. Within thirty years it had become a thriving town, and had taken over from Keswick the role of chief tourist centre.

The next line to penetrate the fells was the Conison branch of the Furness Railway, opened in 1859, built principally to export copper from the mines above the town. Again, the station was far above the town, but as copper production declined, so the line began to encourage slate and timber traffic, and tourism; a group of Furness Railway directors operated a steamer on the lake as early as 1860.

Fig 28 Backbarrow: abortive railway plan 1845

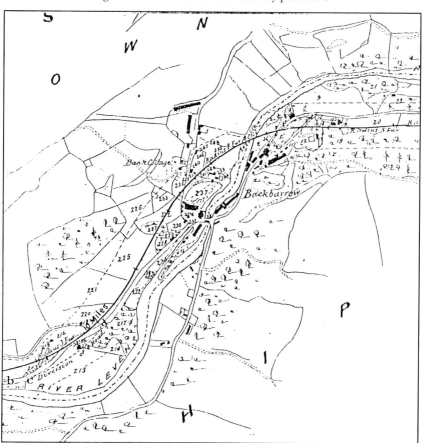

153

The third line into the Lakes was the only one to pass *through* the area; it ran from Cockermouth (which had been linked to Workington since 1847) through Keswick to Penrith, and was opened in 1865. The main reason for building this line was to bring low phosphorous coke from Durham via the line over Stainmore to the iron works of West Cumberland (with a return cargo of iron), but it was routed through Keswick rather than going north of Skiddaw (with its lead and copper mines) in order to tap the tourist market, for Keswick and Borrowdale had traditionally been the prime goal of tourists to the Lakes. Once again an hotel was built near the station and tourism (of a more genteel nature than at Windermere) was quietly encouraged. However, Keswick never became a second Windermere, being so much further from the industrial towns of Lancashire. The line also carried granite, lead, limestone, slate and pit-props, as well as general agricultural produce.

In 1868–9 the Furness Railway opened a branch to Lake Side on Windermere, which both connected with the existing steamer services, and passed very close to the Backbarrow iron works and two gunpowder mills; it also exported bobbins from Stott Park Mill. At Lake Side a lavish station, restaurant and pier were built; the line's most famous early passenger was H. W. Schneider, the Barrow ironmaster, who lived at Bowness, and travelled by steam yacht and train each day to his office.

The final line to be built into the fells was the route from Ravenglass to Boot, opened in 1875, specifically to bring out the rich haematite ores. The line was narrow gauge (3ft) and the cost of moving the ore was reduced by about 80%. Unfortunately, the line soon ran into financial difficulties, and the mining company failed in 1882. After a complicated series of changes, the line was converted to miniature gauge (15in) in 1915–17, and thereafter concentrated on the tourist trade. Of all the lines to penetrate the fells, only this and the Windermere line survive more or less intact.

The other group of lines to be built in the area was the network linking the coal and iron mines behind Whitehaven and Workington. The first line linked Whitehaven with the new ironworks at Cleator Moor as well as with Frizington and Egremont in 1856; mineral lines soon began to lead off in all directions to the various mines, and the main line was extended north to meet the Workington–Cockermouth line in 1866. These lines allowed the development of company towns and villages, notably the planned town of Cleator Moor; whilst the ease of moving the iron ore meant that most later ironworks were built more conveniently on the coast (at Harrington and Workington, for

Plate 35 Little now remains of the railway junction at Rowrah, north of Cleator Moor. Here the line built by the ironmasters met the earlier main line from Cleator Moor to Cockermouth and a branch line ran to the iron mines on Kelton Fell *(Paul Hindle)*

example) rather than on the ore field itself. In only two years (1869–71) the number of iron furnaces in Cumberland doubled from 17 to 34 (see Chapter 5).

This rail network was essentially complete by 1870 but an entirely new and independent set of lines was superimposed from Cleator Moor to Harrington and Workington, as a response to the poor service and rising prices charged by the existing railway company. The new line was largely financed by the iron industry, and it was opened in 1879, with a link to Rowrah (Plate 35) and the Kelton Fell Mineral line opening in 1882. But ore production reached its peak in 1882, and changes in iron making and the working out of some deposits meant that the iron industry soon went into a slow but steady decline; some lines lasted little more than half a century.

However, other routes clearly had tourist potential, and the Lakeside and Coniston lines turned increasingly to this source of revenue. The Furness Railway also encouraged the development of select seaside resorts at Seascale and Grange. At Seascale a grandiose design never came to fruition, the location being too remote. However,

Grange became quite a success as a retirement resort, although it never took off as a centre for family holidays; it was essentially a genteel seaside version of residential Windermere.

Rail closures began in the 1920s and continued through to 1972 with the final closure of the Penrith to Keswick line. Tourism was not the saviour of the railways, chiefly because the companies did not rise to the challenge it presented. Perhaps if the closures had been postponed only a few years, more lines would have survived, for some of the railways once feared by Wordsworth and Ruskin have come to be revered as tourist attractions in their own right.

If many lines were short-lived, their impact on the landscape was immense; within a few years green fields sprouted mines and quarries, with all their buildings and spoil tips. The arrival of the railways allowed the minerals to be mined and then used in industrial processes; mining villages and industrial hamlets sprang up in the landscape, and some settlements such as Aspatria, Harrington, Frizington and Millom grew into sizeable towns. The established towns such as Maryport and Workington grew as well; Whitehaven by contrast was already a town of 20,000 in 1851, and grew more slowly.

The effects of the railways were complex; they did not always allow rural industries to survive, but agriculture benefitted by being able to send milk, butter, cheese and meat to the industrial towns. They allowed local people to migrate out of the Lakes, whilst allowing other workers to migrate in (notably to Cleator Moor); tourist access was meanwhile dramatically improved. They provided employment both in the construction and the running of the lines, yet their impact was concentrated on the industrial development of the mining areas and the ports, to the detriment of much of the rest of the area; in a few years the whole social and economic pattern of life in the Lake District, and more especially around the Lakeland margins, was radically altered.

Little now remains of many lines; some are neglected and overgrown, rapidly disappearing into the landscape, with their station buildings converted into houses, whilst others have suffered the indignity of having roads built over them (notably the Keswick to Cockermouth line). The wheel has now come full circle, and the brief intervention by the railways in the provision of transport in the Lake District is essentially over.

7

VERNACULAR ARCHITECTURE OF THE LAKE DISTRICT

HOWEVER attractive the landscape of the Lake District, it is almost as difficult to picture the scene without buildings as without sheep. Whether as isolated points of punctuation on the hillsides or as the domesticated base from which the wild fells rise, the buildings contribute a visual component to the landscape as well as indicating stages in its evolution. Those humble utilitarian farmhouses and farm buildings which nowadays are called works of vernacular architecture constitute essential evidence in the development of landscape history.

In studies of vernacular buildings generally it has been found convenient to separate farm buildings from the domestic buildings of the farmstead. The houses then may be divided into the categories of Large House, Small House and Cottage according to the assumed social status of the families for whom they were designed. The matter of social status was important not least because of the sheer survival of buildings to populate the landscape. Although the Lake District has been inhabited for so long, the houses of the inhabitants which remain above ground, occupied or ruined, represent only the latest centuries of occupation or the latest generations of inhabitants.

It seems likely that the long-vanished dwellings or farm buildings were made of material too impermanent to survive or of material too valuable not to be used over and over again. Impermanent materials include turf, peat and clay and the seventeenth-century and eighteenth-century clay-walled buildings which do survive on the Solway Plain, just north of the Lake District, suggest that skill in the use of such an abundant material as clay could well have been more widespread. Impermanent materials also include thatch whether of poor oat straw or of heather. Re-usable materials include the stout timber which made up structural frames clad in such materials as clay or turf and also the stone, whether gathered from the fields or roughly quarried near each building site. The redundant halvings and pegholes in timber indicate its re-use; walling stone may be used several times without giving evidence of re-use.

However, the early vernacular buildings which do survive appear fully developed in plan and cross-section and from each early plan-type a full sequence can be seen to have developed. The evidence suggests that in the Lake District, as elsewhere in the country, a Great Rebuilding occurred whereby householders felt sufficiently prosperous and sufficiently self-confident to replace their inadequate dwellings with others stout enough to survive to the present day. As one might expect, those of higher status in a given locality felt able to participate in a Great Rebuilding or enjoy a housing revolution first, while those at the bottom of the local social ladder escaped such benefits until much later. Equally, one finds that at all social levels any Great Rebuilding took place much later in this poor and remote region than it did in more favoured counties such as Kent or Sussex or even Devon or Somerset.

Thus in looking at Large Houses, Small Houses and Cottages we are looking at the evidence in the built landscape of the interaction of social and economic forces as well as those of topography and climate. Different social classes went through similar stages of development in their houses but at different times. Similarly in looking at the agricultural buildings of the farmstead we are seeing another Great Rebuilding reflecting status, albeit of a different sort from that of the domestic buildings. The rebuilding of farm structures tends to be later than domestic structures in the first place, but the benefits of properly planned buildings erected in a permanent fashion went first to the farm buildings of higher status, such as barns and stables, and passed down to those of lower status, such as pigsties and poultry sheds, rather later. Furthermore the buildings show how the tremendous improvement in farming techniques led to a demand for more farm buildings and of even better design and construction than those already provided.

LARGE HOUSES

Large Houses, which were occupied by families of some local importance, survive in some form from the late medieval period, are rather more numerous from the sixteenth and seventeenth century, but merge into the category of polite architecture when built in the late eighteenth century and afterwards. The earlier buildings include some real or fanciful provision for defence, but later examples make no such acknowledgement. Large Houses were also farmhouses and substantial ranges of farm buildings, many of nineteenth century date but some of earlier dates, provide a setting for the domestic buildings.

Isolated towers are not characteristic of the Lake District. More commonly the early Large House was based on a conventional T-shaped or H-shaped plan with one wing taken up as a tower, battlemented and with walls of defensible thickness, and sometimes, as at Beetham Hall near Milnthorpe and Middleton Hall near Kirby Lonsdale, with stone curtain walls and some simple gatehouse. Even these houses are relatively less numerous than in other parts of Cumbria where closer proximity to raiders and more productive land worth more ambitious raiding made provision for defence more understandable.

The T-shaped Large House plan included a multi-storey wing at right angles to a hall which was open to its roof. The more common H-shaped plan made use of two such wings, one at each end of the open hall. The original central hearth heating the hall has in all cases been replaced by a fireplace: a deep chimney breast boldly projecting from the rear wall of the hall, or, more commonly, a wide stone fireplace backing onto the cross-passage which ran between hall and cross-wing. Conventionally there was another passage, running through the lower cross-wing and leading to an outside kitchen, but here the passage was vaulted and flanked by vaulted buttery and pantry, an arrangement which may be seen at Preston Patrick Hall. As elsewhere in the country the hall was usually modified by the insertion of an intermediate floor in the late sixteenth or the seventeenth century and the great chamber so formed was made more modern and more comfortable by the provision of a plaster ceiling which, as at Yanwath Hall near Penrith, conceals the magnificent carpentry of a medieval roof.

Late sixteenth and seventeenth century Large Houses had two main storeys and often an attic and sometimes a basement as well. They were often of a plain rectangular plan shape but with a boldly projecting multi-storey porch. Many rooms were heated and this improvement in comfort was advertised by tall cylindrical stone chimney stacks, the simple northern counterpart to the highly decorated brick chimney stacks of southern England. Large mullioned and transomed windows graced the main elevations and lit rooms decorated with panelling and plasterwork. Most of these houses were one room deep, elongated or rambling, but a small handful were compact and two rooms deep.

With the late seventeenth and the early eighteenth century, traditional plans gave way to symmetrical layouts based on a front door located about the middle of a more or less stylish elevation. A group of houses in West Cumberland, represented by Moresby Hall, presented elaborately rusticated masonry elevations to visitors approaching the front door. More commonly, as at the Wordsworth House in Cockermouth, the rendered walling of the main elevation was picked out in stone dressings.

The Large Houses of the Lake District are charming and picturesque in appearance, but, apart from such ambitious houses as Levens Hall, Sizergh Castle or Askham Hall, they are not in the front ranks of the nation's vernacular architecture. The stone of the heart of the Lake District did not lend itself to architectural embellishment. Original window patterns have been lost in eighteenth and nineteenth century alterations. Impressive spaces have been cut up to make rooms more suitable for the life of the farmer and his family. Nevertheless the Large Houses are an important part of the vernacular architectural scene both in themselves and in the influence they had on design of smaller houses.

SMALL HOUSES

In the Lake District, the Small House of the yeoman or tenant farmers and their social equals emerges fully developed in plan and constructed of permanent materials about the middle of the seventeenth century. At the moment we know very little about their predecessors but the fully mature state of the seventeeth-century plans suggests that a change of building material or construction method rather than a new departure in planning was indicated in the seventeenth century. The reasons for this housing revolution or Great Rebuilding are as obscure here as in the rest of the country though here, as elsewhere, accumulation of capital through advantageous economic conditions presumably was a prerequisite. It may be that social and assumed legal changes following the Union of the Crowns in 1603, and the confirmation of customary tenure with right of inheritance in 1625, led to circumstances in which such a Great Rebuilding could be contemplated and implemented after the days of the Civil War and Commonwealth.

The chief Small House plan types of the seventeenth and early eighteenth century in the Lake District were based on the two units of living and retiring spaces, the expansion of these units longitudinally for service or farming needs, and, less commonly, the use of a plan of three domestic units with back-to-back fireplaces in place of a gable fireplace.

160

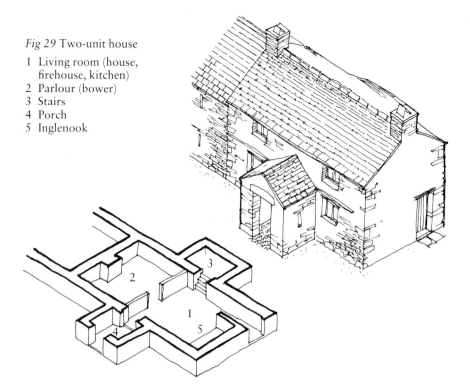

Fig 29 Two-unit house

1 Living room (house,
   firehouse, kitchen)
2 Parlour (bower)
3 Stairs
4 Porch
5 Inglenook

Two-unit houses

At the heart of the two-unit house was the living room, variously called the house, the firehouse, the kitchen etc. and this contained the principal or only hearth or fireplace. Off this room opened a room serving as a parlour or ground floor bedroom. In the earlier and smaller examples this room was unheated; later a gable fireplace was included. A dairy, or similar ventilated storage space, was partitioned off the parlour or was included in a lean-to extending behind the living room. Virtually all surviving examples of the two-unit houses have an intermediate floor, the earlier and smaller buildings having an undivided loft in the roof space, the later and larger farmhouses having quite well-proportioned bedrooms upstairs. A tight winding staircase ran either from the rear of the living room or, rather surprisingly, from out of the parlour. Most commonly, however, the staircase was contained in a deep projection from the rear wall. The main heat source was the open fire burning peat on a hearth-stone in an inglenook. The focus of domestic life and the centre of folk practices and superstitions connected with the house, the inglenook dominated the traditional farmhouse interior until it was superseded by the coal-burning cast-iron range. The upper part of the inglenook was the hooded chimney consisting of a wide flue gathered together in a half-pyramid to join the chimney stack. The

161

Plate 36 Two-unit house *(T. Whittaker)*

hooded chimney was made of studs lined with wattle, clay daub and plaster, and joined a stone chimney stack which was carried on wooden cantilevered beams. In later examples both chimney and stack were made of stone, retaining the original shape but modified to a graceful curve. At one side of the hearth was a stone or timber partition called the 'heck' and this shielded the inglenook from the worst of any draughts coming through an adjacent door. At the other side, the front wall of the house included a small window, the 'fire window', which lit the deep inglenook. The hearth wall usually included a recess which served as a salt or spice cupboard and other recesses or 'keeping holes' for a lamp or the farmer's pipes. Usually the spice cupboard had a carved door but many of these have been removed.

Occasionally houses of this plan were entered through a gable wall but in nearly all the examples now to be seen the main doorway is placed near the centre of the elevation and opens directly into the living room. Only in later centuries, it seems, was a single-storey porch added to help counter the draughts from the winds sweeping in from the fells. The basic plan of the two-unit house was employed until well into the eighteenth century. It met the minimum domestic demands of the small farming family for a more public room for eating and entertaining, a more private room for the master and mistress and for

162

storage of seed corn and fleeces, and some loft space for the children. At the same time the room sizes and the room heights could be increased without altering the plan so that later and more progressive farmers could enjoy a familiar plan in improved form.

Cross-passage and downhouse plan

Like the two-unit plan, the cross-passage and downhouse plan consisted of two main living rooms on the ground floor but in addition there was a substantial service room at one end. A cross-passage ran from the front to the back of the house alongside the wall which contained the principal or only hearth; access to the house was through a doorway in the hearth wall near the end of the cross-passage and by way of a short lobby formed by the heck partition. The cross-passage ran through the 'downhouse' or service room. Normally unheated, the downhouse apparently acted as a scullery, and implement store, a fuel store and brewhouse. In early and small examples it was open to the roof, but in later and larger examples it was lofted to provide a granary or a chamber above, and the cross-passage itself was defined by a timber or masonry partition wall. Eventually the downhouse was provided with a fireplace and became the kitchen. As the front door to the downhouse was also the entrance to the house as a whole it was given

Plate 37 House with cross-passage and a downhouse to the left of the doorway (*T. Whittaker*)

the arched head, moulded jambs or decorative lintel which indicated its importance. *(See below for plan).*

Houses with cross-passage and attached farm buildings: longhouses
The third of the house plans of this Great Rebuilding and one associated with the heart of the Lake District as well as the more populous northern and eastern areas of Cumbria is the longhouse derivative, a version of one of the ancient plan types found in many parts of England and Wales. Here the plan consists of the basic accommodation of the two-unit plan but entry is by way of a cross-passage, not one passing through a domestic service room but through attached farm buildings. They may consist only of a cowhouse with a

Fig 30 Cross-passage and downhouse plan

1 Living room (house, fire-house, kitchen)
2 Parlour (bower)
3 Dairy
4 Stairs
5 Cross-passage
6 Downhouse
7 Inglenook

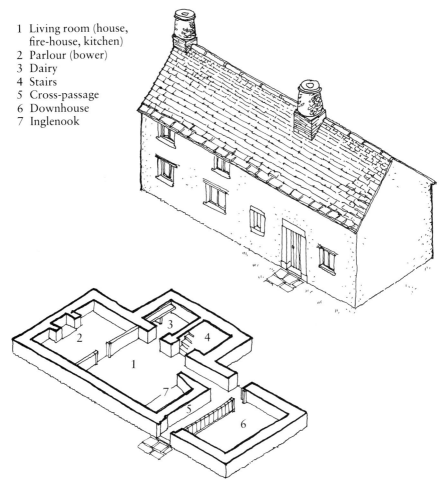

loft above or they may comprise cowhouse, barn and stable. Alterations to both agricultural and domestic portions may obscure the original form though they seem often to respect the original plan. In some cases there still remains some sign of intercommunication between accommodation for animals and humans. Traditionally the cattle reached their stalls by way of the common cross-passage but no surviving example of this arrangement has been discovered in the Lake District.

Houses of the cross-passage plan with attached farm buildings continued to be built until late in the eighteenth century. As in other plan types described, there was a tendency for another front door to be added to the middle of the main elevation of the domestic portion, but this was far from universal. Study of this plan is complicated by the practice, probably a longstanding one, of alternate rebuilding whereby the domestic and agricultural portions of an early longhouse were rebuilt at different times, the line of the cross-passage and the position of the principal hearth remaining constant while everything else changed. It is possible that on an ancient longhouse site the domestic

Fig 31 Cross-passage and attached farm buildings: longhouse

1 Living room (house, fire-house, kitchen)
2 Parlour (bower)
3 Dairy
4 Stairs
5 Cross-passage
6 Cow-house (byre)
7 Inglenook

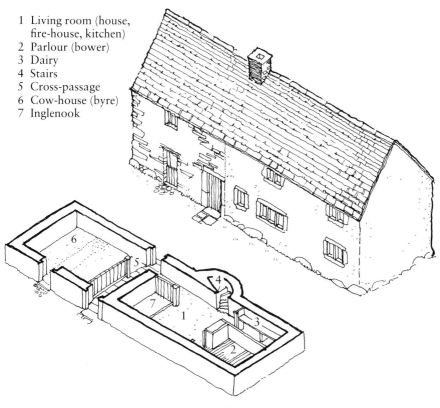

Plate 38 Bridge End Farm, Little Langdale *(T. Whittaker)*

buildings were re-erected in permanent materials first and the farm buildings later, perhaps not until the eighteenth or even the nineteenth century.

Baffle entry houses

A few houses, and those among the larger farmhouses, make use of the baffle entry plan commonly found in Lowland England and Wales. In this the two principal rooms on the ground floor are heated by fireplaces, or from inglenooks, which are placed back to back with entry into a small lobby defined by the jambs of the fireplaces or the hecks of the inglenooks. One room is the main living room and the other usually now serves as a kitchen but may originally have been a heated parlour. Usually there is a third room, an unheated parlour, opening off the living room opposite the fireplace. Houses of the baffle entry plan may be recognised by the great chimney stack rising through the ridge behind the front door.

Houses with rearward extensions

As the Great Rebuilding passed into history, living standards were still increasing and the need for more space, more privacy and more specialised rooms meant that existing farmhouses became inadequate and new houses were built to further developed plans. Increasing the height of the upper storey to provide better bedrooms released the parlour for privacy from the main living room. Extension of the ground floor accommodation longitudinally made for difficulties of

166

access; extension at the rear allowed for neat and compact circulation space.

One way of extending the building was to form a wing at right angles to the house to produce a T-shaped or L-shaped plan on both floors. Another way, more popular, was to add a dairy and a scullery at the rear flanking a generous dogleg or newel staircase and all covered by an extension of the main roof. Locally this is called a 'teufall' roof in allusion to the 'turf-hull' or peat store which was added to the rear of a house when peat was the main fuel. As the fashions developed for taller rooms on the first floor, however, so the height above the ground floor outshut spaces increased and by lofting over these spaces low narrow store rooms were contrived on the upper level, accessible from the landing at the head of the stairs. The side walls of these rooms were increased in height until they could be used as bedrooms but they were still contained in an extension of the main roof and the eaves line at the rear was still substantially lower than that at the front. Externally, apart from the outshut at the rear, such houses were similar in appearance to the later versions of the two-unit plan. There was a front door located about the middle of the elevation but rarely in the exact centre. It was offset so as to give a reasonable balance in the size of the two principal rooms. Windows were equally placed on each side; there was rarely a fire window as the inglenook and hooded chimney had been superseded by the conventional gable fireplace. There were full height windows on the first floor, though internally they were placed quite close to the bedroom floor. The distinguishing characteristic remained the lop-sided appearance of the side elevation with the rear eaves lower than those of the front.

Double pile houses

It needed little further development for the plan with continuous two-storey outshuts at the rear to become the double pile plan which had four rooms on each of two floors. The ridge moved to the centre of the roof as the house as a whole came under one roof and the eaves at the rear were raised to meet the level of the eaves at the front. Partition walls were made substantial enough to carry purlins and no roof truss was necessary. The plan remained satisfactory with little modification until Small Houses were no longer traditionally designed by the second half of the nineteenth century.

Small house plans generally

In looking for house plans one has to remember, of course, that there were houses newly built to the accepted plan for the period and at the same time there were houses adapted or modernised to change from an archaic plan to one more up to date. Changes in masonry technique may indicate that a block has been extended, a wing added, or a storey raised but the exterior of a building does not by any means indicate the full extent of alterations and it is necessary to get behind the plaster and into the roof space of a house if one hopes to identify the stages of development of buildings which may seem to be quite humble.

COTTAGES

In the Lake District the cottager class of landless agricultural labourers, small craftsmen, miners and quarrymen seems to have been small (outside the towns), until the middle of the eighteenth century. Most farms were of small acreage and required little labour beyond that of the family and the practice of boarding the odd labourer or dairymaid survived until quite recently in Cumbria. Hence cottages must have been few and their early planning and construction remained uncertain. However, the industrial and agricultural revolution of the period from about 1750 created a cottager class and a demand for cottage designs. The earliest cottages consisted of one room about 14ft (4.3m) square containing one door, one window and one fireplace. The few surviving examples have a loft in the roof space reached by means of a steep fixed ladder. From this basic plan there were two developments: in one, extra accommodation was provided at the rear to give a larger and a smaller room on each of two floors with a tight staircase included in the rear extension; in the other the extra accommodation was provided alongside to give a double-fronted cottage usually with a very steep staircase between the larger and smaller of the ground floor rooms. These more developed cottage plans may be seen attached to farmhouses of the period or in pairs or little terraces in the villages or near the sites of mines and quarries.

FARM BUILDINGS

Until the scientific design of farmsteads met the demand for improved farm buildings following the agricultural revolution, farm buildings on the larger farms seem to have consisted of scattered individual units, with the cruck-trussed threshing barn the only one of any architectural pretensions and those only slight compared with barns of, say, Essex or West Yorkshire. The small farmer seems to have been content with a cowhouse and loft and a minimal barn attached in some way to his farmhouse. Indeed the practice of attaching some farm building to one end of the house persisted until late in the nineteenth century. From the second half of the eighteenth century, however, farmsteads of more or less regular design were found at both the Large House and the Small House levels. The standard family farmstead of farmhouse, threshing barn, stable, cowhouse and cartshed/granary is to be found in the Lake District as elsewhere in this period.

There is, however, one farm building type which is so well represented in the Lake District as to be recognised as its distinctive building type: the bank barn (Plate 39).

A bank barn is a farm building which combines a conventional threshing barn at an upper level with a cowhouse, stable, cartshed or loose boxes at the lower level. The upper level is reached from the fields, the lower level opens onto the farmyard. The true bank barn is always sited along the contours of a natural or artificial slope though there are variations, found especially in the southern part of the region, in which the barn is placed across the slope. The upper level included a threshing floor, and its big barn doors were usually protected by a canopy and often had projecting wings on each side at the head of the access ramp, while its winnowing door, a small domestic-sized door, was located in the far wall appearing to open precariously to overlook the farmyard below. There were trapdoors through which straw, or later hay, could be dropped to the animals below. At the lower level there was often an open-fronted cartshed immediately under the threshing floor, a cowhouse at one side, and a stable with a taller ceiling at the other. In many examples the doors into these spaces were protected by a continuous cantilevered 'pentise' or canopy allowing the upper part of a split door to be opened for ventilation in the worst of the weather.

Bank barns are very numerous in the Lake District but scarcely found in the other parts of the country in which similar topography and similar climate have produced similar architectural practices. They seem to be typologically related to combination farm buildings to be found in hilly places as widely scattered as Norway, Switzerland and Pennsylvania but there has been no convincing cultural link established to explain the similar designs. In the Lake District they were used for about two hundred years; large buildings probably of this type have been discovered at Rydal and Sockbridge and possibly of seventeenth-century date. Examples are plentiful from the 1730s and the latest dated example is of 1904. The combination of a long low whitewashed farmhouse and a tall dour bank barn may be seen all over the Lake District.

Other farm building types making use of the sloping ground were in-

Plate 39 Bank barns at Troutbeck near Ambleside *(T. Whittaker)*

tended for the storage of hay rather than the threshing of corn. They include variations on the field barn in which storage located partly in a loft and partly in a two-storey 'sink mow' served a cowhouse or loosebox for young cattle in the winter. Many of these buildings are scattered on the fellsides but many are included in farmsteads also. One variation, locally known as the 'hog house', had similar provision but for sheep (hoggs) rather than cattle.

The so-called 'spinning galleries' are to be observed here and there in the Lake District. They are believed to have been intended for the storage, preparation and drying of woollen yarn rather than primarily as a pleasant spot for the spinning wheel – indeed many of them face north. The galleries are sometimes associated with farmhouses but more often they project from the upper levels of bank barns, the floor of the gallery serving as a pentise and the roof being formed by a continuation of the roof of the barn itself.

BUILDING MATERIALS AND CONSTRUCTION

While building form is generated by plan and cross section, building appearance depends on how that form is clothed in walling and roofing materials and these in turn depend on the structural system chosen as their framework. Some buildings are based on cruck construction, others, especially in the towns, are based on post and truss construction while the remainder are of load-bearing wall construction. The roof loads in cruck construction are carried by way of a ridge purlin, side purlins and wall plate onto frames made up of inclined heavy oak timbers joined by a collar or tie beam to make an A shape. The several bays of a cruck-trussed building make up an independent structural frame around which are built walls which in the Lake District are almost invariably of stone; the cruck trusses are not visible on the exterior and it is impossible to say how many apparently conventional stone-walled buildings conceal complete frames of cruck trusses. In later examples wall plates are carried by the walls themselves and purlins are partly carried on gable walls so only intermediate trusses are used. In other late examples upper crucks rise from tie beams which are themselves carried by the solid stone walls. In post and truss construction roof trusses are constructed separately and carried on timber posts which are braced together to ensure stability. Such frames may be clad with plaster or hung slate or may be entirely concealed behind later masonry.

In the heart of the Lake District the hard igneous rocks were used as the main walling material together with the slate-like stones which were quarried, gleaned from the fields or, in the late eighteenth and nineteenth centuries, available as the waste products of the roofing slate quarries. In the inferior buildings, such as the minor farm buildings, these stones were laid dry, that is without mortar, but in most domestic buildings they were laid in a bedding of clay mortar, and they also had a plaster lining inside and sometimes a rendering of many layers of whitewash outside. In some buildings, especially those of the nineteenth century, the slatestones were laid watershot with a tilt to allow any trapped moisture to escape downwards to the outer surface of the wall.

Around the heart of the Lake District there is a ring of Carboniferous Limestone which widens to provide the chief walling material in the southern half of the region. Generally the limestone is found in rough irregular blocks which cannot be made into dressings and sometimes other stones are laid as 'throughs' to help stabilise the walls by tying the outer and inner skins together or are worked into mullions and transomes for the windows and doorheads and jambs for the entrances. However, not all the Carboniferous Limestone is so intractable and the material may be found quite well worked with quoins and fair faced walls. In contrast to the dull sometimes drab olive green of the slate stones the bright limestone, often rendered in later buildings, gives a bright appearance to the Kendal and Furness districts. On the coastal plain to the west and in the Eden Valley to the east, red sandstone is the main building material. It is easily squared and takes mason's work easily though some varieties decay distressingly. Celia Fiennes, the seventeenth-century traveller, was especially enthusiastic about sandstone, believing Penrith to be a town built of the currently fashionable brickwork as she approached its deep red buildings. In all parts of the Lake District one may see the use of cobble stones; they are rounded stones collected from fields and river beds and used for rough walling with other stones to provide a tie, or when split to give a fair face, used as general walling.

Clay construction was widely used in the Solway Plain and a still numerous but sadly diminishing number of examples testifies to the versatility and durability of this material. It is known that the present area in which these buildings are found excludes the parts of north-eastern Cumbria where clay building was once used and it is possible that use of the technique in the Lake District was common enough, notwithstanding an apparent abundance of stone for building.

Although the present-day visitor takes away an image of white-washed houses in his mind and in his camera and although Wordsworth complained about the harshness of whitewash among natural building materials, its use is far from universal even on domestic buildings. Nevertheless whitewash did serve to distinguish the farmhouse from the farm buildings and whitewash does accentuate the entrances running along the base of the farm buildings.

Lake District slate, or 'blue slate' as it was generally called, was widely used in the roof coverings of superior buildings in many parts of the country during the eighteenth century, and superior buildings of the Lake District itself were also covered in the local material. In the nineteenth century, however, Welsh slate became increasingly competitive and became the normal material for use in domestic and industrial buildings except where clay tiles were cheap and plentiful. Even in the Lake District one finds that Welsh slate was quite frequently used, especially when railway lines helped take the coastwise shipments into the heart of the country. Whether locally quarried or imported, slate was often used in place of thatch on the older and humbler buildings. It is hard to accept that thatch was ever an important roofing material in the region but the buildings in the background of the paintings and engravings which helped advertise the Lake District as a tourist resort in the eighteenth and nineteenth centuries appear to have been thatched. The compilers of Directories in the eighteenth and for much of the nineteenth century make clear that, in the countryside, thatch was only just giving way to slates. Thatching seems to have been in a relatively crude technique making use of turf and heather as much as straw or reed. Another roofing material, found more on the fringe than in the heart of the Lake District, was thick sandstone flags. They gave a heavy but stable roof and the lichen-covered flags make an appropriate cover to buildings of sandstone or limestone walls.

Roofing techniques include the use of 'corbie-stepped' or 'crow-stepped' gables. There were few opportunities for virtuosity with any of the local building materials, roofing or walling, but the termination of slated roofs with walls rising up the gable in steps was a popular device from the late seventeenth century onwards. At base and apex a selected or roughly worked stone acted as a finial. Another device still to be seen sometimes was the use of 'wrestler' slates at the ridge. In the absence of stones to be worked into ridge covers, this vulnerable part of the roof was protected by slates cut and slotted tightly together in the manner of wrestlers in the Cumberland and Westmorland style.

Tall cylindrical chimney stacks have already been mentioned in connection with Large Houses of the sixteenth and seventeenth centuries. They are also to be seen in some Small Houses built a century later. They are often found projecting from gable walls, rising from a square base which is carried partly by stone or timber members cantilevered from the gable wall and which, internally, is designed to receive the upper part of a chimney hood rising from an inglenook. Chimney pots are with few exceptions a recent addition. Traditionally the whole chimney top was open even if this meant that there was a 'hallan drop' of sooty rain falling into the inglenook; however, it later became the practice to place a pair of inclined slates at the top of the chimney stack. Because of the vulnerability of chimney stacks to the weather, small stones being exposed to hot smoke and sparks inside and cold rain and snow outside, they often had to be replaced. Quite often, therefore, the chimney stacks are later than the date of the rest of the building.

ARCHITECTURAL DETAILS

To confine observation of the buildings of the Lake District to their planning and construction would be to ignore the devices which helped ensure their architectural delight. Although few buildings, whether domestic or agricultural, reveal the hand of the professional designer, the greater proportion, the vernacular buildings in fact, display the good proportions and the appropriate architectural details which delight both inhabitants and visitors. To a large extent the architectural decoration was dependent on the walling material to hand. Where sandstone was available or could be economically trans-ported moulded jambs, classical architraves and carved ornament could be provided quite easily. In the district around Kendal where Carboniferous Limestone of good quality could be obtained then some dressed work may be seen. In the slatestone districts of the central Lake District, however, decoration comes partly from the few attempts to project stones as if in indication of a label course, or incline long stones in allusion to the lines of a pediment, but mainly from the qualities of the material itself. The openings are quite roughly formed; wooden mullions and transomes give emphasis to what they serve.

Few early windows survive but occasionally, and then perhaps in abandoned buildings or transferred to farm buildings, one may see the stout chamfered wooden jambs, head and sill of unglazed windows protected only by internal shutters. On some of the Large Houses, such as Preston Patrick Hall, there is evidence for the drawbars which secured the shutters at night. Traces of early glazing may sometimes be seen where removable lattices of leaded lights fitted more or less snugly against rebates in wooden jambs, mullions and transomes. Again, traceried window heads surviving here and there show early attention to detail.

During the eighteenth century and the first part of the nineteenth century characteristic window shapes changed from long runs of lights divided by moulded or square-cut mullions or the pairs of lights with a mullion between to the carefully disposed tall windows with dressed stone architraves and sills. At the same time the glazing changed from small square panes set in lead or wood to the rather larger and more carefully proportioned panes of spun or cylinder glass characteristic of the Georgian period. In most surviving examples these are set in verti-cally sliding sashes but in a few instances the old single mullion and transome arrangement divided the window into four segments. The spun glass glints with the arcs of bubbles and other imperfections; the cylinder glass betrays the slightly bowed contour which comes from its manufacture, again catching the light intriguingly. The so-called Yorkshire sliding sash, the poor man's version of the vertically sliding sash, included an opening light sliding horizontally on a wooden bead. Most of these horizontally sliding sashes have three panes in each light. In the latter nineteenth century sheet glass was introduced and the large blank panes spoil the scale of so many traditional buildings into which they have been introduced.

It is always worthwhile to try to look at the sides and rear of a build-ing as well as the front. If the building has been erected at one time the front windows will be up-to-date and those at the side and rear may be of archaic form. Even on the front the windows at the attic and basement level tend to be inferior in quality or earlier in style than those serving the main rooms. Doors have a similar hierarchy; the front door and doorway are up-to-date, the back door and frame may literally be from a previous era.

CONCLUSION

Whether from siting, from planning, from materials and construction or from architectural detailing, the buildings of the Lake District have a character which sets them off from those of other regions. They have a character which invites the visitor to add his own associations to make them a major element in the Lake District experience. Very few of the buildings are great architectural monuments or enshrine occasions or historical memories of great significance. The buildings we mostly observe and appreciate as part of the landscape of the Lake District are truly vernacular. Since the term is generally taken to mean 'of the people and of the place' these traditional buildings to long-tried designs using local materials are well represented in the Lake District. There were few opportunities for professional architects to demonstrate their skills in the regions until quite late in the nineteenth century. However, during the eighteenth century an architect, through family connections, perhaps, might be asked to prepare a 'model' for some work and an up-to-date design might then be imitated by the local masons. The Lake District yeomen had a reputation for education and quite wide reading and so as architectural pattern books began to circulate during the eighteenth century one would expect a receptive even if limited market in the region. Although some of the more remote valleys remained isolated, the larger lakes and the fringes of the Lake District came to be frequently visited. Thus the vernacular content of the buildings began to diminish with the second part of the nineteenth century. Even then the tradition of using local materials persisted so that it was not until well into the twentieth century that the vernacular tradition was completely lost. Now the conservation movement and strict planning controls help to ensure that the traditional buildings survive as far as possible, playing their essential part in the make-up of the Lakeland landscape.

8
NATIONAL PARK LANDSCAPE

IT is now widely acknowledged that the concept of national parks originated in 1810 when William Wordsworth first published his *Guide to the Lakes*. In a much quoted passage he suggested that '. . . persons of pure taste . . . deem the district a sort of national property in which every man has a right and an interest who has an eye to perceive and a heart to enjoy'. However, if the idea was British, the realisation was American for the world's first national park was established at Yellowstone in 1872; seventy-nine years later, in 1951, the Lake District National Park (LDNP) was created. There are, of course, fundamental differences between the American and British parks; in the USA – and internationally – a park must be essentially a wilderness area containing natural landscapes of great beauty or special scientific interest which are unaltered by man. Moreover, these national parks must be owned or managed by the governments concerned. In Britain, none of our ten national parks meets these standards. The word 'national' has, unfortunately, given rise to some basic misconceptions; the parks are neither 'nationalised' nor government owned. There is also considerable public confusion between National Parks and the National Trust; in a recent survey conducted by the Countryside Commission, 50% of those questioned thought that the National Trust controlled Britain's national parks. In effect, the country's parks are 'national' in the sense that they are of special value to the nation; although they are administered by local government, much of the land within the parks is privately owned. In the case of the LDNP almost 25% is owned or controlled by a charity, the National Trust, and 58% is in private hands. All of Britain's national parks are man-made landscapes, the product of the interaction of man and his animals over thousands of years, essentially human landscapes, farmed and forested, drained and dammed, moulded and modified. Yet for all that they are areas of great beauty and the principal aims of the national park authorities (NPA) is to preserve and enhance that beauty and to promote the enjoyment of the parks.

The LDNP encompasses some 880 square miles (2243 sq km), making it the largest of Britain's national parks, an area which includes some of the finest mountain scenery in the country. When measured against the American or European parks, the LDNP seems insignificant, at least in size, but its importance in the cultural history of Britain is considerable; here is a landscape in which eighteenth and nineteenth century romanticism took root and flourished, a spiritual environment which inspired poets, writers and artists such as Wordsworth, Coleridge, Southey, Ruskin, Constable, Turner and, more recently, Norman Nicholson and Melvyn Bragg. Yet it would be wrong to consider the LDNP simply as a preserved 'heritage land-scape' pickled in aspic and, as Norman Nicholson aptly put it, 'smothered in good taste and embalmed in admiration'. It is a living landscape, the home of almost 40,000 people, and the NPA has a responsibility to ensure that the social and economic well-being of those who live and work in the park is safe-guarded. However, to con-serve the characteristic beauty of the park, to promote the enjoyment of the area and to support the social and economic life of the inhabit-ants is a difficult – some would say contradictory – task, yet this is the challenge which confronts the Lake District Special Planning Board.

One of the essential factors in the conservation of the LDNP is the scale of the landscape. It is possible to walk through the park in two or three days, to motor through it in an hour and, as Wordsworth himself pointed out, '. . . from a point between Great Gavel [Gable] and Scawfell, a shepherd would not require more than an hour to descend into any one of eight of the principal vales by which he would be sur-rounded, and all the others lie (with the exception of Haweswater) at but a small distance'. It is precisely this smallness of scale, linked with a great variety of scenery, which makes a landscape of great beauty but, at the same time, one which is vulnerable to disfigurement. A line of electricity pylons marching over the fells, a tall telecommunications mast on the skyline, a multi-storey hotel block or a new reservoir would all be obtrusive and alien features on this landscape. On de-velopments such as these, the LDNP Special Planning Board, consist-ing of representatives from Cumbria County Council, District Councils, and members appointed by the Secretary of State for the En-vironment, keeps a vigilant eye. Indeed, any development which will affect the landscape must be approved by the Board and more than a thousand planning applications are processed each year. Inevitably there are conflicts of interest arising out of competing and sometimes mutually-exclusive uses of land within the park – forestry versus sheep farming, water supply versus farming and tourism, slate quarrying versus landscape conservation, mass tourism versus farming, and of course the NPA is open to criticism of bureaucratic control and authoritarianism. But John Wyatt, the former National Park Head Ranger, has made the valid point that the measure of success of the planning authority is not what one can see but what one cannot see. Similarly, Brian Redhead, the President of the Council for National Parks, has recently suggested that 'National Parks must be seen not as places where nasty things are not allowed to happen, but as places where good things happen'.

CONSERVATION

Long before the LDNP was established, various organisations expressed an interest in the conservation of the Lake District. In 1883 the Lake District Defence Society was formed to oppose further mineral

"Apparently it's the new National Trust - approved footwear, to stop erosion on the fells..."

Fig 32 Courtesy of Colin Shelbourn Westmorland Gazette, *2 November 1987*

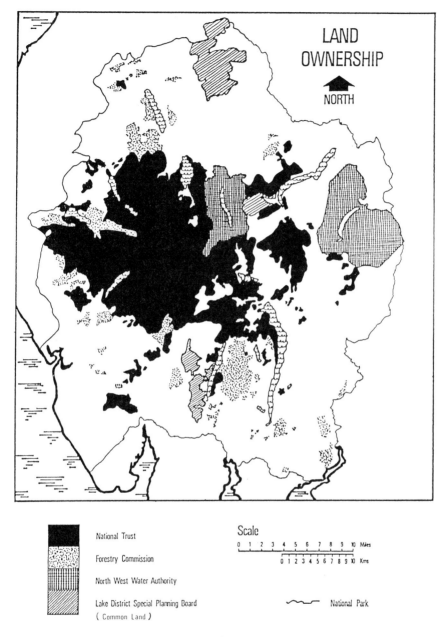

LAND
OWNERSHIP
NORTH

■	National Trust	
▦	Forestry Commission	
▥	North West Water Authority	
▧	Lake District Special Planning Board	
	(Common Land)	

Scale

0 1 2 3 4 5 6 7 8 9 10 Miles
0 1 2 3 4 5 6 7 8 9 10 Kms

～～～ National Park

Fig 33 Land ownership

extraction from the fells and in 1895, under the influence of Canon H.
D. Rawnsley, Vicar of Crosthwaite, the National Trust was founded.
In its early days the Trust was largely a Lake District institution; in
1902 it acquired its first Lake District property, Brandlehow Woods
on the western shores of Derwentwater, followed, four years later, by
Gowbarrow by Ullswater and, in 1908, Manesty was added. The

Fig 34 Nature conservation

generosity of individuals such as Beatrix Potter, Professor G. M. Trevelyan and Sir Samuel Scott further increased the Trust's holdings to the extent that today it is the largest single landowner in the park, controlling nearly a quarter of its area, owning 86 farms and 22,500 sheep (Fig 33). In the 1930s a Lake District Safeguarding Association was formed and, fortunately, changed its name to become the Friends of the Lake District, a vocal and active pressure group. The Cumbria Trust for Nature Conservation has dedicated itself to the preservation

180

of Lakeland wildlife and threatened habitats and it now controls thirteen conservation reserves within the park. In addition, the Nature Conservancy Council has listed seventy-nine Sites of Special Scientific Interest (SSSIs) as well as four National Nature Reserves and two local Nature Reserves. Together, these organisations represent the 'conservationist lobby' within the park. Yet they themselves are not beyond criticism. One President of the National Farmers' Union denounced conservationists as 'braying do-gooders' and, sadly, that is a viewpoint still held by some Lake District farmers. Conservationists are not infallible and mistakes have been made. The partial destruction by default of a terraced mound behind Fell Foot farm, a National Trust property in Little Langdale, thought by some archaeologists to be a 'thingmount' similar to Tynwald Hill on the Isle of Man, was regrettable (Plate 14). Many people felt that the NPA's permission for the construction of a group of wooden buildings to house a water ski school at Lowwood on the shores of Windermere was misguided. Similarly, the chainlink fencing of an SSSI on Armboth Fell, between Thirlmere and Watendlath, sanctioned by the National Trust, the Planning Board and the Nature Conservancy Council in an effort to ease grazing pressure, is now acknowledged to be a considerable embarrassment to the three organisations. But fortunately such lapses are relatively rare and are far outweighed by projects which enhance the landscape – the waymarking and repair of footpaths, the building of bridges and discreetly hidden car parks, the splendid Ranger and National Trust Warden services and the provision of purpose-built information centres. And in the final analysis, a critical question must be posed: 'What would the Lake District landscape have looked like without the conservationist lobby?'.

FARMING

Of all the factors which influence the landscape of the park, farming must necessarily be the most important; not only does it shape the landscape, it is also a significant employer of 2,800 people. Moreover, despite the fact that most farms in the park consist of Grade 4 and 5 land, the Lake District uplands are a reservoir of lambs, store and breeding stock for the lowlands. The pattern of farming within the fells is largely governed by two sets of factors – the physical limitations and the economic climate. The seemingly inflexible physical restrictions are obvious to most visitors – the steep slopes and thin, acid soils mean that a high percentage of land in the park cannot be cultivated and grass crops are restricted to the flat valley floors such as Borrowdale

Plate 40 The farming landscape in a 'less favoured' area. At Wasdale Head the good quality 'inbye' land on the flat valley floor contrasts with the thin, stony, bracken in-fested 'intaks' on the steep fellsides. The drystone walls are not only stone fences enclosing the small, irregular fields, they are also stone dumps created when the 'inbye' land was created by the men, women and children who cleared the land of boulders and stones *(W. Rollinson)*

and Great Langdale (Plate 40). In other areas, for example the low-lying land between Bassenthwaite Lake and Derwentwater, the land is susceptible to flooding and is virtually worthless. High rainfall, often more than 100in (2540mm) a year, together with a corresponding high incidence of cloud, further limits the type of crop grown and de-creases the growing season. In spring, when the fell tops are still under snow, cold air drains down the fellsides and so reduces the length of the growing period. In effect, spring comes late to most of these fell farms; on the lower lands of the Eden Valley, West Cumbria and Low Furness, lambing occurs in February whereas in the fells lambs are usually dropped in April, clearly reflecting the environmental differ-ences. In some of the major valleys, aspect can also influence the farm-ing pattern. In Great Langdale, a deep, glaciated trough orientated east–west, most of the farms are located on the sunny, south- facing slope, above the flood level of the beck; the exception is Side House farm on the north-facing slope which in winter is in the shadow of Side Pike and consequently is known as a 'cold farm'.

Not surprisingly, the physical difficulties and natural handicaps of the Lake District fells qualify the area for livestock subsidies under the EEC's Less Favoured Area (LFA) scheme which aims to conserve the countryside and arrest depopulation by a system of grants. Almost 90% of the area of the park is classified as an LFA and so is eligible to receive headage subsidies for every breeding ewe and cow. Theoretically, the effects of this artificial economic climate should be beneficial, but unfortunately this is not always the reality. Although subsidies provide a welcome source of income for most hill farmers, in some cases they have encouraged an increase in stock and consequent over-grazing of the fells, a reduction of labour and the growth of larger units of production – all at the expense of the environment. It is estimated that between 1975 and 1981 the numbers of sheep and lambs on Lakeland farms increased by 13% to 734,986, clearly reflecting the growth in subsidies. Deterioration of pasture is increasing and some scientists fear a corresponding increase in soil erosion. Furthermore, recent surveys have revealed that most of the subsidies benefit the larger farms on the better marginal land rather than the small farmer working on the margins of cultivation.

To many visitors, the Lake District landscape presents a picture of permanence, a farming landscape which is resistant to change, but such a view is deceptive. Of course, the way in which the land is held remains more or less the same. Most fell farms have three categories of land: a small area of 'inbye' land, relatively flat and close to the farmstead, is the best quality land, kept in good heart by the application of fertiliser; then the 'intak' or intake land on the fellside, being the stony, steep, second quality land, and, finally, the rough moorland and fell tops. The proportion of fell, 'intak' and 'inbye' land varies from farm to farm but Seathwaite Farm at the head of Borrowdale is typical with about 80 acres (32.3 hectares) of 'inbye' and unlimited grazing rights for over 2,000 Herdwick sheep over 2,000 acres (809.2 hectares) of some of the highest fell land in England. However, changes in farming methods and increased mechanisation have had an impact on the landscape. Within the last two decades, the number of family farms has diminished; between 1975 and 1981 some 142 family farms and 104 part-time farms were lost and the figure is currently running at 70 farms lost each year. In essence, this means that many smallholdings and farms are being amalgamated to form more viable units, but this has also resulted in the deterioration and sometimes loss of miles of drystone walls and hedges. A survey undertaken by the Friends of the Lake District in 1985 indicated that in the four parishes of Borrowdale, Ireby, Longsleddale and South Winster, 37 miles (59.5km) of drystone walls and 77 miles (123.8km) of hedgerows have vanished since 1947. In many areas, bracken has invaded the 'intak' land and rushes have infested the 'inbye' pastures; outbuildings and byres have deteriorated, and gaps in walls and hedges have been filled with barbed wire and corrugated-iron sheeting. The increase in decay of such landscape features is indicative of the farmers' inability to afford repairs and maintenance costs; indeed, it might be argued that such features are indicators of the upland economy generally. Recognising the dilemma posed by an apparently decaying landscape within a national park dedicated to encouraging tourism, the Countryside Commission launched an Upland Management Experiment in 1969 to offer farmers financial encouragement to carry out small schemes to improve the appearance of the landscape and to enhance the recreational opportunities of the uplands. The success of the scheme was soon apparent and today the Upland Management Service, now incorporated into the Park Management Department, cares for footpaths, rights of way, repairs to stone walls and bridges as well as conservation projects on farmers' land.

Yet perhaps the greatest threat to the agricultural landscape comes from the fickle nature of the economic climate and in particular the vagaries of the EEC agricultural policy. Traditionally, the upland farms of the Lake District have been a source of sheep for fattening in the lowlands, and this has been encouraged by headage subsidies. Indeed, the extent to which the upland economy depends on sheep sales was emphasised by the aftermath of the Chernobyl disaster when sheep movements within much of the national park were prohibited, resulting in severe hardship for the fell farming community. There are current fears of a collapse of the sheepmeat market which, in turn, could precipitate a crisis in hill farms already dependent on subsidies. Such a disaster would soon find expression on the Lake District landscape – the lowering of the physical boundary of cultivation, the further invasion of 'intak' land by bracken and rushes, the abandonment of smaller farms to holiday 'lets' and second homes and, in all probability, the extension of coniferous forests onto land which once supported sheep. In short, a change in the economic climate could produce a radical alteration of the traditional landscape of the Lake District uplands.

FORESTRY

One of the anomalies of national park legislation is that forestry is not subject to planning controls and this has given rise to some concern not only within the planning boards but also amongst amenity and con-

Plate 41 The coniferisation of the landscape. During the planting of Ennerdale Forest in 1927, some 2,000 Herdwick sheep were displaced from the fellside *(W. Rollinson)*

servationist groups. Of course, friction between the advocates and opponents of afforestation is not new; Wordsworth objected strongly to what he called 'the stern regimentation' of the new plantations and in 1810 he wrote:

> I . . . regret that they should have selected these lovely dales for their vegetable manufactury, when there is so much barren and irreclaimable land in the neighbouring moors.

But following the depletion of woodland for the war effort in 1914–18, the newly formed Forestry Commission pursued a policy of coniferisation of several areas of the Lake District. The result was aesthetically unpleasing; the insistent ruler-straight edges and harsh fire roads, the block planting on bare hillsides and the imposition of a uniform dark blanket of conifers were both unsympathetic and unnatural. Moreover, forestry and sheep farming were virtually mutually exclusive; when the huge Ennerdale Forest (Plate 41) was planted in 1927, some 2,000 Herdwick sheep were excluded from their 'heaf' and similarly some 1,600 sheep were displaced when the Thornthwaite estate was established. In the 1930s, the Friends of the Lake District orchestrated a vigorous campaign against the afforestation of Eskdale and Dunnerdale with some success but the 'economic necessity' argument was difficult to counter. However, under an agreement between the

Forestry Commission and the Council for the Preservation of Rural England, it was decided that some 300 square miles (776.7sq km) of the central Lake District should be free from planting. Half a century later, 'sheep may safely graze' here still without the fear of being displaced by trees – but for how much longer?

Britain is currently one of the least forested countries in Europe and therefore imports more than 90% of its timber needs. Such a situation is seen as undesirable in government circles and an increase in afforestation has been sought. The secondary argument that forestry creates jobs in upland areas is regarded as spurious by some experts since forestry, like agriculture, has become more mechanised and labour intensive. Within the LDNP, the Forestry Commission owns 5.6% of the land area including the great Grizedale, Ennerdale and Thornthwaite forests, but there are also areas of private forest such as the Thirlmere plantations, originally established in the late nineteenth century to protect the reservoir's catchment area. In the early days of its existence, the Forestry Commission concentrated on the production of quick-growing softwood coniferous timber with little regard for the more sensitive environmental issues – the dark, monoculture plantation of the Ennerdale Forest is still an affront to many environmentalists and conservationists. However, since the 1960s there has been a welcome change in the attitude of the Commission to both the landscape and to tourists. A programme of thinning and 'amenity planting' of deciduous trees is softening the much-criticised straight-line planting of the first-generation forests such as Thornthwaite and Bassenthwaite; a new policy to promote broad-leaved woodland has been launched, and visitor centres have been opened. But the show-piece of the Commission is undoubtedly Grizedale Forest, between lakes Windermere and Coniston. Here a system of multiple land use has been successfully introduced; a museum and information centre educate visitors in a gentle but effective way, thousands enjoy the waymarked routes through the forest, including the 9½ mile (15.2km) long Silurian Way. Hides and look-outs make it possible for individuals to see and appreciate wildlife, and open-air sculpture and picnic sites add variety to the forest walks. The Theatre in the Forest, a pioneering venture, attracts artists and performers of national and international standing. Yet, despite the development of its tourist and visitor potential, Grizedale remains an important centre for the production of softwood timber.

Just as upland farming is susceptible to changing economic policies, so, too, forestry is equally exposed to such pressures. The Treasury requires the Forestry Commission to earn a 3% return on its plantations, including those in national parks, and in the light of government stringencies, this target is likely to be increased. Will such a policy result in more and more Norwegian and Sitka spruce being squeezed onto the available land? Furthermore, fears are expressed that future government policy might involve the privatisation of some of the land owned by the Forestry Commission and this has alarmed the conservationist lobby which argues that private forestry companies could constitute a threat to the landscape. Although the tax advantages afforded by private forestry to pop stars, football players and media personalities have recently been modified, there are still suspicions that these private companies are essentially financial institutions with little interest in the aesthetics of landscape. If the depression in upland farming deepens and more marginal land becomes available, will these private forestry groups acquire such land for planting? Certainly government policy would appear to be encouraging such developments for a former Minister of Agriculture, Mr. Michael Jopling MP, whose constituency includes part of the LDNP, has recently said that forestry offers '. . . the most promising alternative for land when no longer required for agricultural production'. Such a policy, if implemented, would have a profound and lasting impact on the Lakeland landscape. And in the event, would a privatised Grizedale or Thornthwaite forest still provide facilities and access for the general public or would the tree crop be the over-riding purpose of the forests to the exclusion of other activities?

WATER SUPPLY

One of the indisputable – and infuriating – facts about the Lake District is the high rainfall; over 120 square miles (310.7 sq km) of the central fells have an annual rainfall of more than 100in (2540mm). A rapid run-off, together with glaciated, U-shaped valleys which, when dammed, form deep but narrow reservoirs high above sea level so that distant towns can be supplied largely by gravity flow, means that this area has an enormous capacity of surplus water. This potential was appreciated as early as 1867 when covetous eyes were cast on Ullswater as a possible source of water for London. The plan did not materialise, but the seeds of the idea had been sown in the minds of the Manchester Corporation Waterworks Committee and in 1876 the city decided to draw water from Thirlmere. The scheme aroused considerable controversy; the Bishop of Manchester suggested that if Thirlmere '. . . had been made by the Almighty expressly to supply the densely populated district of Manchester with pure water, it could not have been more exquisitely designed for the purpose', a view which was vehemently opposed by the Bishop of Carlisle. 'May Cottonopolis be sent nearer home for its water supply . . .' thundered the *Gentleman's Magazine*, '. . . and not interfere with the public pleasure in things on which it has itself never set any value; the solemnity of solitude, the unruffled aspect of nature, the glories of mountain, and the peacefulness of the mere'. But the case was lost and in 1890 Manchester laid the foundation of a dam which raised the water level by 50ft (15.24m) and inundated several farms, the hamlet of Wythburn and its 'inbye' land. Streams from the slopes of Helvellyn were channelled into concrete troughs, coniferous plantations were established to reduce soil erosion and 'No Trespassing' notices were erected. It was not until the second half of the twentieth century that the shores of the former lake were once again opened to public access.

Manchester's second great reservoir scheme, begun in 1929, created the Haweswater reservoir which resulted in the destruction of the community at Mardale, its farms, its inn and the seventeenth century church (Plate 42). In all reservoirs, the unseasonal fluctuation of the water level results in barren, plantless shorelines, particularly in drought conditions; in the summer of 1984 the level of Haweswater was sufficiently low to reveal the remains of the former village of Mardale (Plate 43). For many it was a spectacular and unusual sight; for a few who had lived in the settlement and worshipped in the church it was a sad and poignant occasion.

In the mid-1960s Manchester once again intensified its campaign to extract more water from the Lake District; this time the scheme called for the partial flooding of the beautiful Winster valley, the construction of a pipeline down Longsleddale and the abstraction of water from Windermere and Ullswater. In opposing the plans, the NPA faced their first major test and, incidentally, received widespread public support throughout the country. On paper, the conservationists lost their case, for Manchester was given the power to take water from both Windermere and Ullswater; in practice, however, the strength of opposition clearly brought about a modification of the original plans. No dams were permitted, all pumping stations and straining wells have been constructed under ground, and extraction limits have prevented the 'draw-down' shorelines.

In the late 1970s the alarm bells were triggered once more when the North West Water Authority, Manchester's successor, proposed increased water extraction from Ennerdale and, almost at the same time, British Nuclear Fuels published plans for a new weir and increased flow from Wastwater, Cumbria's wildest and most Scandinavian lake.

Plate 42 Man's impact on the landscape: Haweswater reservoir. The dam was constructed in 1929 and the water level raised by about 95ft; this resulted in the destruction of the hamlet of Mardale with its school, the Dun Bull inn, the seventeenth century church, and four farms. The remains of the church lie between the small island and the wooded peninsula (W. Rollinson)

Plate 43 The 'draw-down' effect at Haweswater reservoir, summer, 1984. The unseasonal fluctuation of the water level prevents the establishment of plant life around the shores of reservoirs. In this view, the walls and field patterns of the destroyed village of Mardale can clearly be seen (W. Rollinson)

The public outrage and opposition to such schemes was overwhelming and, after a lengthy enquiry, the proposals were defeated. In justifying his judgement the inspector gave support to the view that '. . . if it is right that any places in England should remain inviolate, surely Wastwater is one of them'. This and other encouraging signs such as the opening of public access to the shores of Thirlmere promise some hope for the future. During the last fifteen years, water consumption appears to have fallen and some authorities have suggested that the threat of adding to the Lake District's already existing 17 reservoirs is receding. However, the 1986 LDNP plan adds a cautionary note:

> There is no guarantee that a scheme in the national park will not prove to be the cheapest available source of water yet again.

Moreover, if the NWWA is privatised, will the new owners look sympathetically on public access? The answer to this question is of critical importance to the future of the national park.

QUARRYING AND MINERAL EXTRACTION

The removal of minerals and slate from the national park is as emotive and divisive an issue as water extraction. The conservationists would certainly agree with Brian Redhead, when he poses the question 'What is quarrying but the authorised removal of a park?' Yet communities such as Coniston, Langdale and Ambleside still depend to a limited extent on local slate quarries, although this dependence is much less than in the nineteenth century. There are currently eight slate quarries within the park employing a total labour force of approximately 200 people. Of course, the winning of minerals such as lead, copper and silver as well as slate and granite has long been practised within the Cumbrian fells but there has recently been a decline; in 1976 diatomite extraction at Kentmere ceased, followed in 1980 by the closing of the Threlkeld granite quarry and, a year later, by the Carrock Fell wolfram mine. Not surprisingly, these industries have left their mark on the landscape in the form of spoil tips and tailings. In the case of slate quarry waste, vegetation such as lichens, mosses, parsley fern and, later, birch, will colonise the tips, but in other areas such as the spoil produced by the lead mines near Glenridding, the ground is slightly toxic and therefore special treatment and lead-tolerant grasses must be introduced. Some of the disused quarries make valuable and unobtrusive car parks, and at least one, Hodge Close near Tilberthwaite, provides the local mountain rescue team with a splendid man-made cliff face on which to practise climbing techniques.

The very fact that mining and quarrying has been such an important activity in the past means that some of the older workings contribute to the character of the landscape and are part of the industrial heritage of the area. So, does mineral extraction pose a threat to the environment? Once again 'market forces' could be a decisive factor. In the event of a rise in the world market price of copper, wolfram or lead, it is distinctly possible that the large multi-national mining companies would turn their attentions to the Lake District where deposits still exist but, under the present climate, are uneconomic to exploit. Morever, technological developments have made possible the extraction of minerals from waste tips in a manner unthinkable a decade ago; should the price of certain minerals increase, the re-working of old tips could prove economic. But what effect would such developments have on the environment of the park – and should they be allowed? Certainly there would be pressure for the widening and improvement of roads which, in turn, would increase heavy traffic and result in the disruption of life in rural communities. Would the LDSPB be able to withstand the 'national strategic value' argument if put forward by the multi-nationals or even by central government, and would it be able to maintain a case for the prohibition of mining within the national park for minerals that can be found elsewhere? The test is yet to come.

TOURISM

If Wordsworth advanced the first tentative ideas for a national park, he was probably the first to identify the problems associated with mass tourism. His vehement opposition to the Kendal–Windermere railway occasioned a number of letters to the press. In 1844 he complained that:

> . . . the directors of railway companies are always ready to devise entertainments for tempting the humbler classes to leave their homes. Accordingly, for the profit of shareholders and that of the lower class of inn-keepers, we should have wrestling matches, horse and boat races without number, and pot-houses and beer shops would keep pace with these excitements . . . and . . . the Sabbath day in the towns of Bowness and Ambleside, and other parts of the district, would be subject to much additional desecration.

Later in the same century, Ruskin expressed similar views and, in a monumental piece of Victorian paternalism, he wrote of the incoming tourists '. . . I don't want to let them see Helvellyn while they are drunk'. Yet, despite the strictures and reservations of the high minded, the tourists and visitors flocked into the Lake District by rail and later by car. The ease of access, especially by road, has, of course, brought its own problems; it is now estimated that 12 million visitors come to the Lake District each year and that on an average Sunday in summer about 60,000 vehicles most of them on a 'recreational trip', add some 180,000 people to the 50,000 holiday makers already in the area.

Some locations, notably those with access to water, toilets and car parks, are 'honeypots', attracting thousands of visitors on a fine day; the boat landings at Derwentwater, Waterhead near Ambleside, Bowness Bay, Brockhole National Park Visitor Centre, and Tarn Hows, are among the most obvious. But over-crowding is increasingly felt by walkers and climbers; on some days in summer queues develop for the most popular rock climbs. One survey has reported that the summit of Helvellyn, one of the most accessible mountain tops, was visited by 600 people in the course of a summer's day and the total for the week was almost 1,300. Such figures have led one LDNP report to declare that '. . . tourists, by their sheer weight of numbers, are killing what they seek to enjoy'. Yet it is not only enjoyment which is being eroded – the landscape itself is suffering from the geomorphological impact of walking boots and there has been a considerable increase in footpath erosion and gulleying in many parts of the park. Tarn Hows, which receives between half and three-quarters of a million visitors each year, was so seriously affected that the National Trust was obliged to close and re-seed the eroded paths and to lay out a system of new tracks. More recently, the Trust has announced a £12.5 million plan to tackle urgent conservation work on its properties and the NPA has claimed that it is necessary to spend £1 million immediately to clear the backlog of maintenance work on some 1,815 miles (2921.3km) of footpaths and bridleways. Sadly, the problem has been exacerbated recently by the increasing use of scrambler motor cycles on bridle ways such as Garburn and Walna Scar.

Such pressures on the landscape clearly underline the need for some form of management, yet this in itself is a difficult problem. If the increase in seasonal visitors brings problems, it also brings wealth; a recent estimate suggests that the tourist industry in Cumbria is worth £200 million per annum, and plans to restrict traffic in areas such as Great Langdale have met with resistance in the past from those whose livelihood depends on tourism. Most people have now become familiar with the message on radio and television that the Lake District is 'full' at peak periods, so is the answer to create wider roads and more

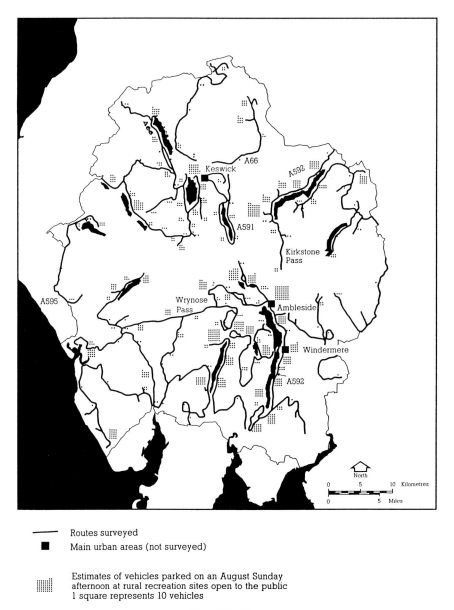

Routes surveyed
Main urban areas (not surveyed)

Estimates of vehicles parked on an August Sunday
afternoon at rural recreation sites open to the public
1 square represents 10 vehicles

Fig 35 Parking

car parks? (Fig 35) The strength of feeling aroused in the 1970s by the
'improvement' of the A66 road and the huge viaduct over the Greta
gorge was considerable, yet, despite alternative plans which would
have linked West Cumbria and the M6 and avoided the park, the route
through the national park was adopted, to the dismay of the conservationists. To many it seemed that the aims of the national park movement had been sacrificed on the altar of expediency. On the question of

193

Plate 44 A Bowness car and coach park during a summer weekend. Are we turning the Lake District National Park into a National Car Park? *(W. Rollinson)*

car parks, the NPA has declared that the criteria must be that they can be integrated into the landscape and certainly the efforts of the National Trust at places like Tarn Hows have been exemplary. There are currently 130 public car parks within the national park offering some 8,500 parking spaces. Is there scope for any further expansion and if so, would we not be in danger of turning the national park into a National Car Park?

If the roads are crowded, so, too, is Windermere. The competition for the use of water space has intensified considerably during the last two decades. It is hardly surprising that the power boat enthusiasts and the water skiing fraternity do not live amicably with the anglers, the swimmers and those who simply wish to enjoy a peaceful picnic on lake shores. Deciding in favour of the quieter recreational activities, the NPA proposed by-laws which, when accepted in 1974, prohibited the use of the smaller lakes for power boating. Nine years later, 10mph speed limits were in force on Coniston Water, Derwentwater and Ullswater, and while power boating and water skiing is still allowed on Windermere, all craft now have to be licensed.

The affluence of some sectors of the public has encouraged the growth of a new landscape phenomenon – the time-share leisure complexes with their restaurants, health clubs and swimming pools often utilising former industrial properties such as the ultramarine works at

Backbarrow and the former gunpowder works in Langdale. Obviously these developments bring wealth and employment to the park and, in keeping with the principle of promoting enjoyment, the NPA has given passive encouragement to such schemes. But there are some dissenters; Ann and Malcolm MacEwen have recently queried whether or not '. . . it [is] really in the spirit of the national park to be "offering a holiday in the Caribbean, a tropical dream come true . . . where you can sip your drinks under the palm trees"'. What, one wonders, would have been the reaction of William Wordsworth or, indeed, of John Dower, G. M. Trevelyan and H. D. Rawnsley?

Some of the problems besetting the national park are social rather than environmental – the 'second home' question, the migration of younger people from the park which in turn leads to the closure of schools because of falling rolls, the increase in the number of retired residents, the decrease in the number of 'service shops' in the face of takeovers by souvenir sellers, and the decline of public transport. Such issues are of paramount importance to people living and working in the park and there are those who would argue that if solutions are not found to these problems, then the concept of national parks will founder. But it might also be argued that if the Lake District is to retain its unique character and fulfil its role as one of Britain's most important national parks, then the environmental dilemmas must also be tackled. It is too easy to conclude that the park is sinking under a mass of problems; there are, in fact, encouraging developments. Joint ventures in land management at Rydal Woods and White Moss Common between the NPA and the National Trust, or at Thirlmere between the NPA and the North West Water Authority, are exciting schemes which point the way to a brighter and more cooperative approach to environmental problems. Brockhole, the national park visitor centre near Windermere, continues to enlighten and educate both adults and children in a new awareness of the life and landscape of the Lake District and many of its 100,000 annual visitors would agree with Norman Nicholson's view that the Lake District National Park is 'more than a convalescent home for sick civilisation'. It is a place for spiritual renewal and refreshment but '. . . to see the Lakes clearly . . . we must penetrate the living landscape behind the view. We must get out of our cars, feel the rock under our feet, breathe the Cumbrian air, and learn to know something, at least, of the complex organic life of grass, herb and tree, something of the changing pattern of weather, water and rock, and something of the way man has helped to shape the landscape in the past and is shaping it today.'

195

BIBLIOGRAPHY

Abbreviations:
Arch. Journal = Archaelogical Journal; CW = Transactions of the Cumberland and Westmorland Antiquarian and Archaeological Society; NS = New Series

Chapter 1
Clare, T., *Archaeological Sites of the Lake District* (Ashbourne, 1981)
Evans, J. G., *The Environment of Early Man in the British Isles* (London, 1975)
Fell, C. I., *Early Settlement in the Lake Counties* (London, 1972)
Higham, N., *The Northern Counties to AD1000* (Harlow, 1986)
Pearsall, W. H. & Pennington, W., *The Lake District: A Landscape History* (London, 1973)

Chapter 2
Clack, P. & Haselgrove, S., *Rural Settlement in the Roman North* (Durham, 1981)
Higham, N. J., (Ed.), *The Changing Past* (Manchester, 1979)
Higham, N.J. & Jones, G. D. B., 'Frontier, Fort and Farmers' Arch. Journal 132 (1975), 16-53
Jarrett, M. G., *Maryport, Cumbria: A Roman Fort and Its Garrison* (Kendal, 1976)
Jones, G. D. B., The North-western Interface, pp93-106 in Fowler P. J., *Recent Work in Rural Archaeology* (Bradford-upon-Avon, 1975)
Jones, G. D. B., 'The Solway Frontier', *Britannia* 13 (1982), 282-97
Jones, G. D. B. & Shotter, D. C. A., *Roman Lancaster* (Manchester, 1988)
McCarthy, M. R., *Carlisle, A Frontier City* (Carlisle, 1980)
Potter, T. W., *The Romans in North-west England* (Kendal, 1979)
Shotter, D. C. A., *Roman North-west England* (Lancaster, 1984)

Chapter 3
Bailey, Richard N., *Viking Age Sculpture in Northern England* (London, 1980)
Baldwin, John R. & Whyte, Ian D., (Eds) *The Scandinavians in Cumbria* (Edinburgh Scottish Society for Northern Studies, 1985)
Higham, N. J., 'Continuity Studies in the 1st millenium AD in North Cumbria', *Northern History* 14 (1978) 1-18

Chapter 4
Bouch, C. M. L. & Jones, G. P., *The Lake Counties 1500–1830: A Social and Economic History* (Manchester, 1961)
Marshall, J. D. & Walton, J. K., *The Lake Counties from 1830 to the mid-twentieth century* (Manchester, 1981)
Nicholson, N., *The Lakers*, (London, 1955)
Rollinson, W., *Lakeland Walls* (Clapham, 1969)
Winchester, A. J. L., *Landscape and Society in Medieval Cumbria* (Edinburgh, 1987)

Chapter 5
Adams, J., *Mines of the Lake District Fells* (Clapham, 1988)
Davies-Shiel, M., *Watermills of Cumbria* (1978)
Fell, A., *The Early Iron Industry of Furness and District* (1908)
Geddes, R. S., *Burlington Blue-Grey* (1975)
Holland, E. G., *Coniston Copper – a history* (1988)
Marshall, J. D., *Furness and the Industrial Revolution* (1958, reprinted)
Marshall, J. D. & Davies-Shiel, M., *The Industrial Archaeology of the Lake Counties* (1977)
Millward, R. & Robinson, A., *The Lake District* (1970)
Postlethwaite, J., *Mines and Mining in the English Lake District* (1913)
Rollinson, W., *Life and Tradition in the Lake District* (1974)
Shaw, W. T., *Mining in the Lake Counties* (1970)
Somervell, J., *Water-power Mills of South Westmorland* (1930)

Chapter 6
Curwen, J. F., 'The Lancaster Canal' CW XVII (1917) 26-47
Hadfield, C. & Biddle, G., *The Canals of North West England* (1970) 2 vols
Hindle, B. P., *Maps for Local History* (1988)
Hindle, B. P., *Roads and Trackways of the Lake District* (Moorland, 1984)
Marshall, J. D. & Walton, J. K., *The Lake Counties from 1830 to the mid-twentieth century* (1981)
Marshall, J. D. & Davies-Shiel, M., *The Industrial Archaeology of the Lake Counties* (1969, reprinted 1977)
Marshall, J. D., *Furness and the Industrial Revolution* (1958, reprinted 1981)
Richmond, I. A., 'The Roman Road from Ambleside to Ravenglass' CW XLIX (1949) 14-31
Ross, P., 'The Roman Road north of Low Borrow Bridge, to Brougham Castle' CW XX (1920) 1-15
Williams, L.A., *Road Transport in Cumbria in the Nineteenth Century* (1975)

Chapter 7
Brunskill, R. W., *Vernacular Architecture of the Lake Counties* (London, 1974)
Tyson, B., 'Mansion House, Eamont Bridge, Cumbria . . .', *Transactions of the Ancient Monuments Society*, NS Vol 31 (1987)
Tyson, B., 'Low Park Barn, Rydal: the reconstruction of a farm building in Westmorland in the seventeenth century', CW LXXIX (1979)
Tyson, B., 'Rydal Hall Farmyard: the development of a Westmorland farmstead before 1700', CW LXXX (1980)
Tyson, B., 'Some traditional buildings in the Troutbeck Valley: a documentary study', CW LXXXII (1982)
Tyson, B., 'Building work at Sockbridge Hall, its farmstead and neighbourhood', CW LXXXIII (1983)

Chapter 8
Berry, G. & Beard, G., *The Lake District: A Century of Conservation* (Edinburgh, 1980)
MacEwen, A. & M., *Greenprints for the Countryside* (London, 1987)
Nicholson, N., 'Looking at the Lakes' in National Park Guide Number 6, HMSO (London, 1975)
Redhead, B., *National Parks Today*, issue 19 (Cheltenham, 1987)
Rollinson, W., *A History of Man in the Lake District* (London, 1967)
Shoard, M., *The Theft of the Countryside* (London, 1980)
The Lake District National Park Plan (Kendal, 1986)
Wordsworth, W., *Guide to the Lakes*, 5th ed, (London, 1835)
Wyatt, J., *The Lake District National Park* (Exeter & London, 1987)

INDEX